DWELLERS AT THE SOURCE

DWELLERS AT THE SOURCE

UNIVERSITY OF

NEW MEXICO

PRESS

Albuquerque

Southwestern Indian Photographs
of A.C. Vroman, 1895-1904
by William Webb and Robert A. Weinstein

ACKNOWLEDGMENTS

The authors are deeply indebted to the Board of Governors and the director, Giles W. Mead, of the Natural History Museum of Los Angeles County which holds the A. C. Vroman Collection. Their making the collection available to us for study is indicative of their approval and support of this project.

Of great practical assistance was the active cooperation of the History Division staff of the museum: Dr. Harry Kelsey, Chief Curator of History; Mr. William M. Mason, Archivist; Mr. John Cahoon, Photo Archivist; and Mr. John Dewar.

The negative collection of the Southwest Museum was made available through the cooperation of Dr. Carl S. Dentzel, Director, and Bruce Bryan, Chief Curator.

Mrs. Hazel Wiedmann, A. C. Vroman's niece, provided us with much useful information, permitted us to make reproductions from a few of the original Vroman platinum prints in her possession, and loaned us the two notebooks that Vroman made on his travels in 1895 and 1897.

Mr. Sudworth Sheldon, manager of Vroman's of Pasadena, ransacked his files for Vroman material and turned up the negative from which we have made our frontispiece as well as other material that has been of considerable help in researching Mr. Vroman's life.

Craig Carpenter read the manuscript and, with his extended knowledge and his own Indian background, was able to offer many very helpful suggestions.

Roger Moss provided useful information concerning the Navajo and Hopi textiles.

Ansel Adams reviewed portions of the text and made many valuable suggestions that have helped us to understand certain stylistic and technical aspects of Vroman's work.

Lilian de Cock provided us with a set of the playing cards that Vroman had published to help awaken interest in the Southwest Indians. The cards proved to be of considerable help in making identifications of some of the negatives.

For other contributions we wish to express thanks to Mr. Daniel W. Jones of Project 20, National Broadcasting Company; Dorothy Jeakins; Charles Rozaire; Robert Ariss; Alan Kishbaugh; David M. Weinstein; and Edwin H. Carpenter of the Henry E. Huntington Library.

A BELATED DEDICATION

When we think about the Indian photographs of Adam Clark Vroman, something altogether startling is suddenly revealed to us: there are no pictures of inscrutable savages! And therein lies a profound difference from so much of the photography of his period. There is no sensationalism, no deliberate portrayal of squalor, no sentimentalism, no propaganda.

The editors of this book are persuaded that Vroman approached the Indians of the Southwest with the intention of portraying them as human beings, not as objects to be described in scientific journals, not as curiosities to be exploited commercially or for personal aggrandizement: simply as human beings.

It is because of this approach, and because of the superb craftsmanship he brought to the task, that his photography speaks so vividly today. In these photographs people communicate with us across the barriers of time, language, and cultural difference. With no falseness between us and the images of these faces, we are exposed so vividly to the humanity of a people that the roots of our common identity are perceived immediately.

Had the arts of communication and of printing and reproduction of photographs been as sophisticated in Vroman's time as they are in ours, and had his photographs been as widely seen then as they can be today, the history of the Indians in the Southwest and the whites who stood against them in ugly confrontation might have been radically different.

Vroman did the best he could to realize such a purpose in his work, to change that history for the better by introducing us to the real people who were being affected. It is with a renewal of that same dedication that we offer this book of Vroman's Indian photographs. We are hopeful that the presentation of these images to a newer and more enlightened generation may contribute to the fulfillment of the vision of all men to live on this planet in harmony with each other, with all other life, and with the earth that was given us.

William Webb
Robert A. Weinstein

CONTENTS

1 | ADAM CLARK VROMAN: AN APPRECIATION

Glasscock and Vroman Bookstore. 60 East Colorado Street. Pasadena, California. Vroman at right. 1895.

A. C. Vroman Bookstore. Interior. Approximately 1900.

ADAM CLARK VROMAN was at different times a railroad man, a fine-book collector and successful book merchant, an amateur archaeologist and historian of the American Southwest, a distinguished collector of Orientalia and Southwest Indian artifacts, a public-spirited citizen of note, and a serious photographer of uncommon sensitivity. A fine bookstore bearing his name still operates in Pasadena, California, and his personal collection of Japanese netsuke is in the Metropolitan Museum in New York City. But it is as an artist-photographer that he is most likely to be remembered.

As far as is now known, Vroman photographed actively for about fifteen years. It was during only ten of these years, 1895 to 1904, that he produced his most important photographs. It is not known what impelled him or who urged him to study photography, or where and when he learned his skill.

Any assessment of an artist is difficult. His sources of creativity are always obscure, and we know far too little of Adam Clark Vroman to make the search, in his case, an easy one. Although his life included many wide ranging interests, concerns he pursued with energy and competence, the scant record offers us only the barest outlines of a complex but interesting human being.

He was born in La Salle, Illinois, on April 15, 1856, of Dutch parents who had moved from New York City to Illinois in 1835. Except that he attended the Illinois public schools little is known of his boyhood. In 1874, his eighteenth year, he began employment with the Chicago, Burlington and Quincy Railroad in La Salle; by 1892 he was in charge of the railroad ticket office.

In that year Vroman married Esther H. Griest, a

victim of early tuberculosis. The couple moved to Rockford, Illinois, where Vroman continued his railroad career. Hoping to find a climate in which his young bride's health would improve, they moved to Pasadena, California, arriving there early in 1892. Her health declined rapidly, and Vroman brought her back to her birthplace, Flora Dale, Pennsylvania, where she died in September, 1894.

In November of that year Vroman opened a book, stationery, and photo-supply shop in Pasadena, in partnership with J. D. Glasscock. The shop prospered quickly, making it possible for Vroman to take his first trip to the Indian country of Arizona and New Mexico in the summer of 1895. He photographed extensively on that trip as well as on seven other trips to the same area between 1897 and 1904.

During those years he made other photographic trips to Yosemite National Park, to all of the Spanish Missions in California, and to the eastern United States, including Washington, D.C.; Rockford, Illinois; and Flora Dale, Pennsylvania.

Vroman toured Japan in 1903 and 1909, photographing and collecting choice Japanese art. In 1912 he toured Europe, photographing French châteaux in the Loire Valley and Rhine castles in Germany. His touring ended in 1914 with visits to the Canadian Rockies and the East Coast of the United States. Shortly thereafter he began a lingering battle with cancer, a struggle that ended with his death at the home of a business colleague, George Howell, in Altadena, California, on July 24, 1916.

He left an estate valued at close to $100,000, which he generously distributed to his family, friends, and employees. The Southwest Museum received much of his valued collection of Indian artifacts, including especially significant examples of both old Navajo weaving and kachina dolls. To the Pasadena Public Library he donated a large and well-chosen California collection; a sum of $10,000 to augment the collection; and a hand-bound, sixteen-volume set of platinotypes from his negatives.

These bare facts of A. C. Vroman's life tell little about him except that he was a successful businessman with a highly developed appreciation for the artifacts of vanished cultures. He was a man of sensitivity and education, at home in the drawing rooms of his time. He preferred intellectual company, enjoyed fine books, and collected netsuke. He was well traveled and enjoyed the "finer things of life." His distinction for us is that he produced a collection of photographs, the largest part of them of Southwest Indians, uncommon in vision and astonishing in execution.

Clearly, this limited recital cannot satisfy our desire to understand more about the sources of Vroman's abundant creativity. There is more to this man than an accumulation of refined sensitivities. What further subtleties, what additional complexities of personality and motivation lie hidden that would, if revealed, deepen our understanding?

An examination of his photographs reveals that the plight of the Southwest Indians affected him greatly. The inherent grace and calm dignity with which these oppressed Indians struggled for a decent life appealed strongly to Vroman's humanitarian instincts. Perhaps equally, his egalitarian beliefs were affronted by the indifference, the neglect, and the suppression with which these people were forced to live and die.

Vroman was not the first photographer in the United States to photograph Indians, nor was he even the first photographer to focus his talents so consistently on the Southwest Indians. He was, perhaps, the *only* photographer who worked among the Indians in the Arizona and New Mexican desert who found there all the human and aesthetic stimulation he needed to produce a body of work of substantial and enduring value. It was there, among the Indians of the pueblos and the mesas, that Adam Clark Vroman found the opportunity he needed to focus his full life's energy in an enduring creative act.

Any survey of efforts by photographers in the United States to make pictures among Indians reveals the conflict in attitudes between the photographer and his subjects. An appreciation of Vroman's work thus rests properly on at least some understanding of that series of complex Indian-white relationships. The accumulation of historical confrontations called the "Indian problem" in the United States is the tap root of such an investigation.

THE INDIAN AND THE WHITE MAN

Most non-Indians living in the United States at the close of the nineteenth century believed that the "Indian problem" had been solved finally, once and for all. Roughly two and one half centuries of slowly diminishing Indian resistance to white penetration and seizure of Indian tribal lands had come to its bloody end. This tragic trail led through many brutal relocations westward from the Indians' ancestral homes on the eastern seaboard, marked by recurring wanton violence such as at Sand Creek, Washita, and Fort Sumner. The white massacre of the Sioux at Wounded Knee, South Dakota, in 1890 symbolized the final broken dream of the Northern Plains Indians to win back both their birthright—their land—and their right to live in their ancient ways.

The massacre symbolized as well the inability of Indians in the United States to resist violence with violence.

For the American Indian the day of the feathered lance, the arrow, and the war club was at an end. For the white majority the bullet, the artillery shell, and the cavalry saber were being replaced by the Congressional committee, the political investigation, the all-important budget appropriation, and the Bureau of Indian Affairs. The time had arrived in the affairs of the white nation to recast political and economic oppression of the Indian minority into a more permanent and more effective mold, and, now that the military struggle for their subjugation was practically at an end, the Bureau's task was the assimilation of American Indians into dominant white culture.

By 1900 North American Indians were divided among themselves. Their ability to defend themselves effectively against the new bureaucracy was almost nonexistent, and bewilderment and despair were spreading rapidly among the tribes. Stunned into apathy by widespread poverty, hunger, and disease, they faced a new dilemma with increasing bitterness. What road would lead them into an honorable and fruitful future? Was the only road one clouded over by the evident determination of the United States Bureau of Indian Affairs to remake Indians into acceptable red "white men," or was a more honorable option open: the continuation of the struggle to maintain the old tribal values? For many Indians, virtually prisoners on their own ancient lands, the path to a hopeful future was both bleak and uncertain. For others the road to assimilation among white men, the road that led to becoming "white redmen," or good Indians, was increasingly tempting.

The policies of the U.S. Bureau of Indian Affairs allowed *only one choice*—assimilation—and the bureau attempted to make pariahs of those Indians who sought to remain true to their ancient tribal traditions.

The work of the Bureau proved to be complex, difficult, and endlessly troublesome for all concerned. Ancient and fiercely held tribal hostilities among some tribes proved almost impossible for white Government agents to understand. Conflicting and overlapping land claims, made more puzzling by numberless layers of broken treaties, rendered fair and equitable judgment to the Indians virtually impossible. Permissible levels of official corruption, bigotry, and brutality on the part of both white and some few Indian officials helped stir accumulated Indian angers into cynical fury.

The zeal of Christian and Mormon missionaries added to the problem. The missionaries' proselytizing energies added little needed fire and brimstone to the Bureau of Indian Affairs' campaign to wipe out Indian religious life. A series of Bureau rulings begun in 1900 effectively suppressed Indian ceremonials for twenty years. There is bitter irony in the fact that American descendants of European immigrants who fled their homelands in the seventeenth century to escape religious persecution, to find and to found religious freedom in a new land, should so energetically deny it to the Indians they found living there.

Indian communities had next to endure the invasion of anthropologists, whose "scientific" questions and methods were too often seen by the Indians under examination as humiliating and hostile.

The anthropologists, because of their professional training, were probably less ethnocentric than any other white groups in the United States and their impact upon the Indians less grievous. Nevertheless, anthropologists, with somewhat dulled responses to Indian sensitivities, prevailed upon the Indians' decency and hospitality to discover and report all they could of the intimate life of a people they believed was about to vanish or be successfully assimilated. In their zeal to study Indian life as completely as possible, certain of them seemed to lose sight altogether of the Indian's right to human treatment. While they wrote with great thoroughness and in objective scientific prose of Indian religious rites, they seemed never to have truly understood the full meaning of the words "sacred" and "privacy," even though such offenses against Indian privacy were frequently unconscious. Wholesale excavating of Indian burial sites was characteristic of this scientific blindness. It is precisely in their white ethnocentric beliefs and in their feelings of white superiority that their conduct can be explained.

With the acceptance of the "white man's burden" concept by the majority of whites, buttressed by evangelical pressures of organized religion, it became easy for almost all white men to regard the Indian simply as an object of curiosity. It was virtually impossible for many white people to regard the Indian as another human being of equal value to themselves. From regarding the Indian as an object of scientific curiosity it was but a small step to regarding him as an object to be improved upon, and his improvement became the official conceit of the Bureau of Indian Affairs. Those who stood to gain in any way from this official conceit approved the Bureau's work and policies. To most Indians such a view was unendurable.

The pressures generated by the Bureau's assimilationist policies were humiliating and frustrating to many Indians throughout the United States, especially the Indians of the Southwest. The Navajo, Zuñi, Hopi, and the several groups of Rio Grande Indians, all dwellers of the Southwest's high, arid deserts, were some of the principal targets of the Bureau's efforts. The uncompromising Apaches and their leaders remained stubbornly unwilling either to listen to or believe *anything* the white man had to say.

Protected by the intimidating desert, living in ancient stone pueblos high on rocky mesas, many Southwest Indians traced continuous possession of their tribal lands back through centuries. The Indians living in both Acoma and Oraibi speak of their villages as the oldest continuously inhabited cities on the North American continent. All of them had lived in fulfilling harmony with the land since their ancestors had first come there. They loved their lands and had lived on them through good seasons and bad before the white men were known.

It was into this calm and harmonious life that the Spaniards, the first white intruders, ventured on their probing expeditions north from Mexico. Although the land the Spaniards called New Spain was not theirs to rename, the Indians who lived there were more than willing to share it and its meager but sufficient largesse with the newcomers. But as the full weight of Spanish religious bigotry was felt, it awakened anger and hostility that flamed into violence. Spanish disrespect for Indian religions was ferocious in its consequences. Invading Spanish priests and soldiers brutally destroyed everything they considered heretical or hostile to the true Christian faith. Nothing was sacred: they destroyed the Indians' sacred places and their holiest objects; they suppressed their sacred dances, rites, and ceremonies. Indian religious practices were forbidden in favor of the "true Christian faith."

In matters of religion, the Indians had always given generously and borrowed freely. A contest between religions or any type of religious war was unknown among them, for religion meant to them a celebration of the eternal mystery of life and the gifts that supported it. The experience was universal, to be shared by all men, each in his own way. Had Christianity contented itself simply with enriching the variety of possible expressions for this reverence, it might even have been welcomed. Indian resistance to Spanish religious fanaticism was inevitable, its violence forseeable. The Indian Pueblo Revolt in 1680, savage and successful, drove the Spanish from Indian lands.

In time the Spaniards returned and evidenced new understanding of how to deal with Southwest Indians. They rooted their foundling communities once more among the Rio Grande pueblos and villages, building their church-forts with greater discretion. This Spanish reconquest, more limited in its success than earlier savage efforts, nevertheless brought additional problems for the Indians. Although the new Spanish influence was slight among the Hopi and the Zuñi, suppression of Indian ceremonials and Indian religious practices continued as a dominant Spanish effort, one that achieved a certain degree of success. But while the Catholic Church, protected by Spanish arms, existed tenuously in the western pueblos, the Indians continued to practice their ancient rituals underground, in secret, evidence that their religious beliefs and practices were *never* successfully replaced by Christianity.

The willingness of the Rio Grande Indians to share their vast knowledge of desert living secured the success of the second Spanish effort. These patient Indians had learned through centuries the unique skills necessary to sustain life in the Southwest desert. In gentleness these Indians taught all their hard-won secrets to the Spaniards. They taught them how to build adobe structures, to dry chili peppers, to preserve meat in the destructive sun, and to make clay ollas to keep drinking water cool in the desert heat. They shared with the Spaniards all the skills of corn agriculture, even the know-how of desert irrigation, crucial to desert dwellers. In their human grace these Indians held back nothing that might help the invaders of their lands.

The ensuing years brought little relief from outside pressures: instead the difficulties increased. Crossing, recrossing, and settling on ancient tribal lands, many Europeans, principally priests and soldiers, urged the pueblo and mesa dwellers to embrace the new "Christian" life. Most of the Southwest tribes rejected the repeated efforts, sometimes openly, sometimes silently, but always in an atmosphere of growing suspicion.

The middle years of the nineteenth century brought land-hungry Americans onto the tribal grounds. They brought their churches, their traders, their stores, their soldiers, and their diseases. They brought their laws, their courts, their guilts, and an unquestionable belief in their superiority, both as whites and as Americans. Energized by their faith in Manifest Destiny, the lust of these fast-spreading Americans for Indian lands continued to keep the tribes in turmoil. As the Indians alternated between short bursts of armed resistance to the Americans and growing despair at their brutal power, the rich spirituality of Southwest Indian life began to disintegrate. The breakup of the old ways was accelerated by the vigor with which the Bureau of Indian Affairs implemented its policies of forced assimilation.

Although vigorously defended by its supporters, in particular by religious interests and land speculators, the Bureau came under increasing criticism. Steady streams of reports of misconduct and abuse in the Bureau's treatment of its Indian charges in the Southwest stirred considerable demand for reform and for sympathetic understanding of the Indian point of view. These demands heightened growing concern for Indian rights among certain white Americans, and the outlines for an effective national movement in support of Indian rights and Indian needs began to emerge at last. These small groups of citizens were awakened by Helen Hunt Jackson's brilliant document, *A Century of Dishonor,* published in 1881, and angered into action by the national success in 1884 of her second Indian work, the novel *Ramona.* Both works angrily detailed the abuses and outrages the Indians were forced to endure.

If there was any timidity about some Southern Californians following Helen Hunt Jackson's lead, vigorous agitation in defense of the Southwest Indians by fiery young Charles Fletcher Lummis swept it aside. A man of powerful enthusiasms, keenly sensitive to Indian oppression, Lummis quickly emerged as a leading critic of the United States Bureau of Indian Affairs. Making use of his association with Theodore Roosevelt, Lummis undertook to further the President's sympathetic understanding of the Southwest Indians. This effort culminated in the publication by Lummis, in the April and October, 1903, issues of his magazine, *Out West,* of a series of articles entitled "Bullying the Moqui." They constituted a bold and forthright attack on the Government's Indian policies and demanded a formal investigation of the conduct of Charles E. Burton, superintendent and disbursing agent for Hopis and Navajos at Keams Canyon in Arizona. The articles castigated Burton for his alleged mistreatment of Hopi schoolchildren, mistreatment that included kickings, beatings, whippings, and threats with six-shooters to assure school attendance. The investigation was secured, and its outcome, although inconclusive, did accelerate the growing national demand for changes in the public policies and covert practices of the Bureau of Indian Affairs.

In Southern California, Lummis' dynamism quickly led to the organization of small groups of men and women determined to advance new understanding and new consideration for the Indians of the Southwest. Among the most effectively persuasive of these reformers were A. C. Vroman's friends, Peter G. and Beatrice Gates. It was indeed natural that many of the most sensitive and compassionate spirits in the small Southern Californian communities would be drawn to such humanist aspirations. They reflected the militant idealism of many Utopian-minded individuals and groups that settled in Southern California in the 1870s and 1880s. Lending themselves to causes from Theosophy to socialism, these Southern California radicals injected vigorous life into efforts to assist the Southwest Indians.

A. C. Vroman knew many of these people in Pasadena and shared their dedication to the Southwest Indians. Out of this dedication was to come Vroman's most eloquent personal statement. His chosen language was photography, to which he brought special gifts. Only a tough and firm spirit combined with his sensitive insights and a personality moved by deep human compassion could have produced the vivid and enduring body of Southwest Indian photographs that is his principal legacy. The simple fact is that art and life were happily joined in this quiet, talented man. His photographs of these neglected and oppressed Indians suggest that for him the taking of such pictures was a deliberate choice that brought added meaning to his life.

Vroman was only one of a long line of men who spent much of their energies photographing Indians. Only an examination of their records, which cover a period of forty-five years, can help us see Vroman's work adequately. Many of these men produced superb Indian photographs earning their rightful place in photographic fame. Vroman's distinction is that *he, more than any other Indian photographer we know,* better resolved the many problems, both technical and human, of photographing Indians as *human beings.* This was done at a time and under circumstances that presented exceptional obstacles. Indians at Vroman's time found it very difficult, understandably, to share their deepest responses with white people. Vroman's photographs reveal his remarkable ability to relate to them in spite of the impediments to such understanding. In this respect Vroman seems to tower over all other Indian photographers in the United States, regardless of the merit of their images.

THE INDIAN AND THE PHOTOGRAPHER

The announcement in Paris in 1839 of the discovery of photography, specifically the daguerreotype process, energized a world impatient to master the new process and create the new and exciting "sun pictures." No subject, no known geographical location, no event, and very few people were safe from the lens of the ever present daguerreotypist. Everything that might be photographed in natural light was fair game, and for the nineteenth-century traveler the believable pictorial record of the new "mirror with a memory" surpassed all other graphic images in popularity.

Introduced into the United States in 1840, the daguerreotype captured on silver-plated copper many aspects of the struggling infant country. The Native Americans were a subject of great preoccupation by white settlers, and interest in them, mixed with apprehension, was very high. There were few early communities in the young United States that did not face, however obliquely, many problems of accommodation with the Indian majority.

At first there was a keen, mutual curiosity between Indian and white man, assuring friendly and willing cooperation between artist and subject. This agreeable mutuality was short-lived. The gathering hostility and violence between Indians and whites that accompanied the initial expansion of the westward frontier inexorably diminished the opportunities for white photographers to work amicably among the Indians. It is to be regretted that, as the technical means for providing a brilliant and vivid record of Indian life finally became available to the photographer, conditions of Indian life had so deteriorated that what remains is, for the most part, a visual record of a harassed, defeated, and degraded people.

John Plumbe at his St. Louis gallery in 1843, Josiah Gregg on the Santa Fe Trail in 1846, Robert H. Vance in Northern California in 1849, and J. Wesley Jones in the early 1840s were making daguerreotypes of the Indians in and from the West. The year 1853 found John Mix Stanley photographing Western Indians and S. N. Carvalho, the official photographer (daguerreotypist) for John Charles Frémont, making Indian portraits and views as well. In St. Louis, gateway to the Western plains, John H. Fitzgibbon was making Indian portraits at his gallery during the mid-1850s. Only the merest handful of these priceless daguerreotype images are believed to have survived the neglect and the indifference of succeeding generations.

The testimony of these earliest photographers all suggest an astonishing degree of cooperation and friendliness by their Indian subjects, a spirit of willingness and trust that seems inexplicable today. When it is considered that contacts with white men among the Plains and Western Indians were sparse at the time, Indian reserve and suspicion under such conditions would have been altogether understandable. Consider as well the impact of a photographic process that was explained as something that manipulated the sun to produce an image of a living person, an image that when looked at neither spoke nor moved. Such an explanation came very close to challenging deeply held Indian beliefs about the ultimate nature of the sun. It is most remarkable that, in spite of such apprehensions, this "white man's magic" was initially accepted by many Indians.

The photographer's ability to "use" the sun in making daguerreotypes was deeply puzzling to many Indians. They were not reluctant to ponder the proffered "scientific" explanation, but they continued to regard with mixed suspicion and awe any person apparently able to manage the sun's activity for personal benefit. The Indians' understanding of the photographer's work is best summed up in their name for photographers: "shadow-catchers." They applied this name to persons who, with the powerful sun's assistance, were able to capture and transfix shadows, as photographers apparently did in making photographic portraits and views. Such portraits were sometimes considered by Indians as symbols of death. The Indian's hesitancy toward relinquishing his image to the control of another person or, more seriously, to a stranger or an enemy, and his profound apprehension toward allowing his wife and children, the most defenseless of all, to be photographed, was almost always misunderstood or disregarded by "scientific" white photographers.

The trust between photographer and Indian in the 1840s and 1850s was a high-water mark. With the exception of a few individual relationships it was never seen again.

The relative calm of that period was followed by a turbulent rush of white men flocking to the Western frontiers. Among the many land-hungry settlers and gold-seeking miners were some photographers seeking new images and a new life on the raw frontier. Perhaps the best known among the photographers was the distinguished American landscape painter, Albert Bierstadt, who with his colleague S. F. Frost practiced photography in the West in 1859, just prior to the Civil War. During that engulfing war the visits of Eastern photographers to the Western Indians were brought to a virtual close.

During the War continuing treaty discussions with selected Indian leaders in Washington, D.C. enabled the Mathew Brady studio, Alexander Gardner, and A. Z. Shindler to photograph, among them, almost all the visiting Indian emissaries. The work of these three photographers survives as a splendid record. It includes the earliest-known photographs of the Chippewa leader Hole-in-the-Day, the Brulé Sioux leader Iron Nation, and the Yankton Sioux leader Struck-by-a-Bee.

The end of the Civil War and the final opening of the West in 1869 with the completion of the transcontinental railroad brought additional photographers to the frontier. Released from their wartime duties, certain distinguished members of Mathew Brady's photographic group found their way west, making photographs of the territory as they came.

At this early date the photographer was limited by the relatively primitive equipment and photographic supplies then commercially available. Lenses, wet-plate emulsions,

and printing papers were much slower in their responses than the materials available to Vroman after 1895. The fact that certain of these photographic artists produced works of great distinction during the 1870s must be credited to exceptional competence and zeal. Photographic images of astonishing visual power, readily accomplished by the photographers of the eighties and the nineties, were something of a technical tour de force for the pioneer photographer of twenty years earlier.

John Garbutt and T. J. Hine photographed among the Pawnee Indians in 1866, antedating William Henry Jackson's superior work among the same Indians in 1869. Alexander Gardner came west to photograph life on the Kansas frontier in the fall of 1867. In 1868 he produced memorable portraits of several chiefs and warriors among the Crow, the Cheyenne, the Arapaho, and the Sioux in attendance at the Fort Laramie Peace Council. It is known that the Gardner portraits included Spotted Tail and Swift Bear of the Brulé Sioux, Man-Afraid-of-His-Horses of the Oglalla Sioux, and Tall Mandan and Two Kettles. The indomitable Red Cloud of the Oglalla Sioux, although present at Fort Laramie in 1868 would not permit himself to be photographed. His refusal at that time was symptomatic of the faltering of the Indian's initial attitude of cooperation and trust toward the photographer. In May, 1870, Captain D.C. Poole of the United States Twenty-second Infantry and agent for the Brulé Sioux took Spotted Tail and others to Washington, D.C., for consultation. In his book *Among the Sioux of Dakota,* Captain Poole notes, "The party refused to visit a photographer and be photographed. Spotted Tail, with all his intelligence, was Indian enough to say that he considered it bad medicine to sit for a picture, meaning that it would bring him bad luck; and whatever he said was followed by the others." Note the reversal in attitude on the part of Spotted Tail in the two years since he willingly posed for Alexander Gardner at Fort Laramie in 1868.

Although relations between Indians and whites were deteriorating and hostility and mistrust was on the rise at the close of the 1860s, another decade would still provide opportunities for effective photographic work among the Indians. The 1870s would allow photographers to produce the largest serious body of historic and ethnological Indian photographs ever taken, noticeably more than any other preceding ten-year period.

It must be stressed that the truly remarkable work of these frontier photographers of the 1870s can *only* be properly understood in the light of the limitations of their equipment and supplies. Using wet plate collodion negatives, first invented in 1851, photographers had to coat fragile sheets of carefully polished glass with a series of chemical solutions. The light-sensitive plate that resulted, wet and sticky from the collodion, needed to be exposed in the camera immediately. The physical fatigue caused by transporting and setting up eighty bulky pounds of photographic equipment on unfamiliar and inhospitable terrain can only be imagined. It was at best no stimulant to renewed fervor. The quality of work produced by pioneer photographers laboring under such conditions is an enduring monument to their determination and their abilities.

Unforgettable are the Indian photographs of John K. Hillers, who accompanied the John Wesley Powell expeditions of 1871–73 down the untamed Colorado River. Equally vivid are the images by Timothy H. O'Sullivan, the immortal Civil War photographer who worked widely among the Mojave, the Zuñi, the Navajo, the Coyotero Apache, the Ute, and the Jicarilla Apache as the official photographer for several U.S. Government surveys under Lieutenant George Montague Wheeler. The magnificent glass plates of Indian life made in the 1870s by William Henry Jackson survive now as photographic legends, so exciting are they in visual grandeur. Other important survey photographers, all of whom photographed Indians, include William Pywell, who went with General Stanley to the Yellowstone in 1873; W. H. Illingworth, who accompanied General George A. Custer to the Black Hills in 1874, and R. Benecke, official photographer for the Newton-Jenney Expedition into the Black Hills in 1875.

Exceptionally fine photographs of Southern Plains Indians and their life during this important decade were made by William Stinson Soule at Fort Sill in Oklahoma Territory. Northern Plains Indian photographers included Stanley J. Morrow of Yankton in Dakota Territory; David F. Barry, who had studios both in Bismarck and at Fort Bufford; Orlando Goff of Yankton; Frank Jay Haynes, who operated a studio at Bismarck in the Dakota Territory; and L. A. Huffman, the most important Indian photographer in Montana Territory. Huffman photographed among the Crow, the Northern Cheyenne, and the Sioux. His work includes "first" portraits of the great Sioux warrior Rain-in-the-Face, as well as the Chief Crow King. Christian Barthemless, a soldier-photographer in the U.S. cavalry, also produced a number of splendid Indian photographs.

Working in the Southwest among the Pueblo, Rio Grande, and Apache Indians were A. Frank Randall; Camillus Fly of Tombstone, Arizona; and Ben Wittick of Santa Fe, with whom Vroman exchanged prints and attended many Indian ceremonies.

Photographers working among the Indians faced many different problems. The Indians' attitudes toward photographers reflected their developing attitudes toward the encroaching white man. Indians were continually forced to face the many-sided pressures of advancing settlers and builders as well as the puzzling and often hostile social and legal views being enforced against them by white men and their armies.

The Indians' original willingness to attempt to accommodate and coexist with whites had by 1870 deteriorated into open bitterness and anger. This hostility of the Indians was actively expressed in raiding parties and in their resistance to white mistreatment in the form of deadly and effective guerrilla warfare. Frontier photographers were often undeserving victims of this disintegrating social order. Identified by the Indians with the United States Army, whose protection the photographer sometimes sought, they frequently found themselves the targets of accumulated Indian suspicion and mistrust. In addition, many photographers, encouraged by their customers to provide photographs of the then popular "good" Indian or "sideshow" Indian, quickly lost such esteem and goodwill they may have built up among Indian leaders, men who demanded respect and understanding from their white "brothers."

In such an atmosphere it is surprising to find surviving bodies of photographic work among Indians, by such men as Will Soule, William Henry Jackson, and A. C. Vroman, that quite clearly indicate a certain degree of trust and rapport between the participants. It is in the extent and the depth of trust between Vroman and the Southwest Indians that mark him and his photographs as unique.

By the end of the nineteenth century, successful Santa Fe Railroad propaganda and spreading curiosity about Southwest Indian life had combined to make travel and visits to homes of Indians living there a popular tourist diversion. The Indians to be seen included Hopis, Zuñis, Navajos, and those in several different pueblos along the Rio Grande in New Mexico between Albuquerque and Taos. Although the land was rough and hotel accommodations and eating facilities scant, the number of visitors to the Indian villages increased steadily. The country was described by Vroman with charming brevity in "Photography in the Great Southwest" (*Photo-Era,* January, 1901): "This entire country from the Colorado-Utah-Nevada line to the Mexican border is a continuous line of pueblo and cliff ruins and is the archaeological wonderland of this country. Hundreds of ruins are scattered over the land, from the Rio Grande on the east to the Colorado River on the west, and for the amateur photographer it is the long looked-for land of opportunities."

Whites considered the Indian towns and their inhabitants especially photogenic subjects, and many of Vroman's photographer contemporaries came to these rocky pueblos to record the life of the Indians living there.

Nothing was overlooked: they photographed Indian customs, religious ceremonies and rituals, sacred dances, and detailed minutae of their daily lives. The most important photographers among Vroman's contemporaries were George Wharton James; Charles F. Lummis; H. R. Voth, a Mennonite missionary living among the Hopis; A. Frank Randall; Ben Wittick; Frederick Monsen; Fred H. Maude; and Sumner Matteson.

The photographer Ben Wittick, a great friend of the Hopis, died from a rattlesnake bite, fulfilling a prophecy made years before, to which Wittick often referred. Invited by a Hopi priest to watch a secret snake ritual, he had been warned of his death by one of the Hopi elders present at the ritual who resented a white man's presence there: "He has not been initiated! Death will come to him from the fangs of our little brothers!" The fatal bite occurred while Wittick was packing a rattlesnake for shipment to his Hopi friends.

Picture-taking in the United States was not merely a pleasant diversion in 1900 but had become a near mania among those able to afford it. Kodakery, or the filling of photo albums with snapshots, became a national custom. The written diary was being replaced with the visual diary. Photography had become a big business, and the making of pictures had become an absolute must for tourists. At the pueblos and on the mesas it was no longer limited merely to the professional or even to the serious amateur, and the taking of snapshots by hordes of curious tourists added new dimensions to old and vexing problems for the Indians. The impact of this craze upon the Indians of the Southwest was humiliating and degrading. The manic fervor of the tourists to get a "good shot" of Pueblo Indian life was so intense that normal, simple courtesies and decent amenities of social intercourse were all but forgotten.

The conduct of some particularly determined tourist photographers, like some inveterate "camera bugs" of today, was especially disgraceful. They openly invaded the Indian's privacy, insulting him by their indifference to his pride and dignity. On occasion they invaded the Indians' sacred places, the kivas, photographing and handling holy objects, and frequently they ignored the restrictions on photographing the *most* sacred dances and ceremonies.

Even some of the professed friends of the Indians, men who should have known better, proved to be a source of difficulty. George Wharton James, an English journalist,

author, and lecturer, and a skillful and talented photographer, was once strongly reprimanded by Vroman for invading a sacred Hopi kiva, unannounced and uninvited.

In an essay written for *Photographer of the Southwest,* photographic historian Beaumont Newhall commented on this problem: "Most tourists . . . in their greed to get pictures . . . changed the life of the Indian by paying him to pose and making him so self-conscious that he even changed his ceremonies. By 1902 Hopi Indians of the Pueblo of Oraibi had restricted photographers to a single area during the snake dance." George Wharton James, writing in "Camera Craft" in November, 1902, described his own actions and those of some of his fellow photographers at a snake dance. Note his comments on the restrictions imposed on white photographers by the Hopi. "This . . . was an innovation. Hitherto every man had chosen his own field and moved to and fro wherever he liked—in front of his neighbor or someone else, kicking down another fellow's tripod and sticking his elbow in the next fellow's lens. Half a dozen or more Indian policemen kept us in line, so we had to go ahead and make the best of it." Imagine such a scene, should it ever occur during Easter Mass in a Catholic cathedral or in a Jewish temple during the high-holiday celebrations.

Among the Southwest Indians there were additional reasons for their reluctance to allow themselves and their ceremonies to be photographed. Spanish suppression of their religious life had forced them to carry it on underground and in secret. It must be remembered that the greatest part of what these Indians did, what they ate, and the clothes they wore all had religious significance. Only in understanding this can the tension in maintaining their religious life underground alongside the public display of their Christian conversion be appreciated.

Under American domination no real change occurred in this area of their lives. The Bureau of Indian Affairs' ruling in the 1900s suppressing native religious life *once more* forced the Indians into secretiveness. Official punishment for disobedience was swift and severe, and Indians quickly learned to be suspicious of most whites who wished to see their ceremonies. White photographers posed a special kind of danger to the maintenance of secret Indian religious life. The possibility that such photographs might be used against them as evidence in a hearing may have occurred to the Indians. Fearful of Bureau reprisals, Indians forbade photographers entrance to certain ceremonies, kivas, councils, and sacred areas. Those photographers who ignored the tribal bans and violated the Indians' religious privacy served only to increase the wariness with which the Indians regarded all white men with cameras: tourists, amateurs, or professional photographers.

In spite of Indian bans on certain kinds of photographs, some white men continually sought ways to photograph forbidden subjects. They seemed to be indifferent to the affront and disrespect their conduct indicated to sensitive Indians.

This curious white insensitivity to the Indian, the failure to render him the respect to which *any* human being is decently entitled, mars the photographic work of many of Vroman's contemporaries. Although these photographers produced images of high documentary quality, almost all of them seem to show overconcern for the spectacular, the picturesque, and the romantic. The search for the romantic, and for "typical" white values in Pueblo Indian life, tended to obscure opportunities readily available for any photographer to present these Indians honestly: they were too ready to cast them in preconceived molds to please dominant white attitudes about Indians.

By contrast the profound human concerns and exceptional insights displayed in Vroman's Indian photographs establish the special worth of his work. Consider these Indians, too often betrayed and mistreated to give their trust to any white man, cooperating with Vroman to produce photographs of empathy, mutual trust, and mutual respect. This is why one finds in his Indian photographs consistently strong evidence of a remarkable human relationship between the photographer and his Indian subjects, all the more remarkable in that it existed in the early 1900s, when the patronizing view of the American Indian was solidly established among white Americans. Vroman's determination to photograph and present the human values of Southwest Indians, to affirm them with grace and strength in his work, was unique.

Study the faces in Vroman's Indian portraits; try to discern even one instance where suspicion or hostility is betrayed in a glance, a posture, or a gesture. In an almost uncanny way, every subject in these photographs appears to *relate* sympathetically to the photographer, to participate actively, as if it were just as important to the Indians that the photograph be a success as it was to the photographer. In this atmosphere of relaxed confidence, possible *only* where mutual respect is operative, Vroman penetrated beyond the surface to present an image of the people's innermost selves.

Vroman consciously avoided the use of the Indian's hard lives to create stereotypes, to deepen racial myths, or to degrade the Indian's social and economic position any further. In "The Moki Pueblos" (*Photo-Era,* February, 1901) he wrote, "The Indian is a sympathetic fellow, ap-

Roughing it in Hopi Country. Mr. H. E. Hoopes and Mr. J. G. Kuhrts with Vroman at left. 1902.

16

preciates kindness, and never forgets a friend. I have no liking for the man who has been among the Indians and says that 'all good Indians are dead Indians,' and for those who have never been among them and hold such opinons, a summer's outing among the Pueblos will, I am sure, bring on a change of heart. I speak only for the Pueblo Indians as I know nothing of the Plains Indians, but have no fear but he will average with us in honor and truthfulness."

Beaumont Newhall, in *Photographer of the Southwest*, published in 1961, considered Vroman's work fundamentally documentary—photographs made largely for their informational value. This judgment suggests that such photographs have value limited to the mere compilation of data, and may overlook their capacity to create a strong emotional and aesthetic response in the viewer.

Is not the worth of a photograph, despite how informative it may be, its power to inspire us, to sensitize us to a wider experience of the world we inhabit?

Vroman's deeply felt concern for the plight of his Indian friends, struggling valiantly to preserve some shred of human dignity while victims of an oppressive conqueror, certainly would have led him to make a record of their condition. And his camera would allow him to gather information which could be marshalled in a persuasive way to present to his contemporaries. Yet, by bringing to this task an enormous dedication and commitment, and allowing his finely tuned aesthetic sensibility, and his considerable technical skills to inform his photographs, he transcended the more mundane aspects of information gathering.

If, through some disposition to classify and thereby limit our perceptions, we use terms like "documentary," or "journalistic," or "artistic," we may be missing the message. The Vroman work would appear to embrace and surround these limiting categories. His work is too rich in aesthetic values, as well as informative values, to limit a description of his legacy to "documentary." And we should view the work, not through the confines of definitions, but as a whole, allowing the richness and many levels of meaning to reach us, and to move us.

Vroman himself appears to have been unconcerned about his "place," or what kind of photographer he was. He had a task before him, call it what you will, and into that task he poured his considerable energy. He seems not to have cared about the celebrations of the local camera clubs. He competed for no ribbons. If he had aesthetic pretensions about his photography, they certainly are not evident in the work. There seem to be no clichés, no hackneyed treatments, no posturing or pandering.

Perhaps it is the unswerving integrity of the work that could mislead one into thinking it lacked an "aesthetic" impulse. If that were so, it would be very difficult to explain how after so many years these photographs retain the capacity to exalt, and to trouble us as profoundly as they do!

VROMAN'S PHOTOGRAPHIC STYLE

At the time Vroman was photographing in the Southwest there was a great deal of activity in photography, taken very seriously as Art, on both sides of the Atlantic. Numerous periodicals kept photographers abreast of one another's work and carried reviews and articles about the many salons where art photographs were being shown. The photographers who participated in this vociferous movement were mainly of romantic temperament. As early as 1860 they had broken away from the "straight" image, the use of photography to record accurate detail resonant with the optical vision of the human eye. They sought to make photography into an Art Form and naïvely assumed that if the product were sufficiently obscure, suggestive instead of precise, they would be fulfilling that lofty ideal. They were powerfully influenced by such painters as Whistler and the symbolists, and they consciously imitated them. But the results of this imitation, which we know today as pictorialism, were sad, ludicrous, banal. Forcing themselves away from the purity of the optical image, they betrayed the very essence of photography. Yet the painters of the time were able to evaluate photography for what it really was. Threatened, but at the same time challenged, the painters, many of them, turned to photography themselves. Others, now liberated by the camera from the confining disciplines of accurate representation, moved toward more imaginative uses of their talents and founded such styles as abstraction, impressionism, and expressionism.

On the other hand, the photographers who continued to work in straight images were much less inclined to consider themselves artists. For the most part they were commercial men, making photographs for sale. In the United States, as the immense spaces of the West were being opened for settlement, a deep hunger for solid information about the new territories developed throughout the East. Information that was believable, that gave a realistic representation of the potentials to be found, that contained no veneer of false romance, was to be found in the straight photograph. Energetic and talented photographers were quick to respond to the new opportunities, soon penetrating deeply into all parts of the West.

On route to the Hopi towns. 1902.

Carrying their bulky cameras and portable darkrooms to the very tops of the mountains or the depths of the canyons, they recorded the West as they saw it, and their images sold readily in the eager market for stereopticon views, post cards, and luxurious railroad brochures. The straighter the image, the more honest and genuine it was, the more it was in demand. To have submitted these images to gum-bichromate treatment or to have tampered in any other way with their pristine directness not only would have been totally inappropriate to the content of the pictures but would have ruined them for any possible sale—perhaps a more important consideration.

We are moved by these images today because of their lack of any pretension whatsoever. We recognize them as art, uncapitalized, in that they are sensitive visualizations conveying the insights gained from earnest workmanship confronting a natural grandeur. We come to appreciate the fact that trying to be Rembrandt might just be a conceit that will derail one's whole effort.

The Western photographer seemed little bothered by the petty squabbles of the pictorialists. Rough and ready men that they were, the kind of issue raised by Peter Henry Emerson, that the photograph must be a faithful representation, must have seemed a statement of the patently obvious, and not worth all the fuss it caused. Nor were these photographers concerned about whether or not they were "artists." It is remarkable, therefore, that Vroman, newly out of the East, no doubt acquainted with the various movements in the arts, deeply sensitive to and involved with things of beauty, should have been similarly aloof, and should similarly have adopted, evidently without experimentation, the straight photographic style in his work. It is most difficult to imagine that he would approach photography in any other way than as a means of creating some kind of beauty. He had no commercial interest whatsoever in practicing photography, and it is quite unlikely that the objectives of the pictorialists were unknown to him, or that he was ignorant of their work. He was, after all, the proprietor of a Kodak agency in his bookstore and could not possibly have escaped seeing the prevailing work of the time. The most likely explanation is that he understood fully what was going on in the world of photography and that he made his choice. That choice would be consistent with his love of the genuine, a trait reflected in everything he did and throughout his collections of netsuke, fine books, and kachina dolls.

But such a choice forms only a portion of the complex that we call a style. The artist inevitably infuses his work with the attitudes of his time, his station in life, and his deeply personal attitudes as well. Vroman's work, especially his earliest, reflects the imposition of the attitudes of his period. His later photographs demonstrate a transformation, followed by the emergence of a more individual and personal concern, and his work becomes richer as a result.

In the period at the end of the last century in the Far West an abundant optimism prevailed among the dominant middle-class. With its vast resources waiting to be harvested, and the seemingly endless prospects for growth, the West came to symbolize a future secure and full of promise. The dark undercurrents of repressed minorities, the poor in the cities, the Indians dispossessed of their lands, the huge destruction caused by lumbering or mining operations—these were inconsistent with the vision of the

Golden Age, to be sure, but they now seemed amenable to change in a relaxed and comfortable notion of progress that would leave no aspect of the human condition unbenefited.

The painters of this period, far more than the photographers whose business was information, reflected the smug self-satisfaction of the middle class of this period. People wanted to admire themselves: they wished for the artist to hold up a mirror to them that would give them pleasure and conceal from the view any blemishes or disturbing tensions. The art of self-admiration thus confines itself to static forms, compositions of equilibrium and symmetry, subject matter that is genteel, idyllic, or antiseptic. If the blandness of such imagery gets to be altogether boring, a little violence, carefully manicured, can be inserted. Violence must be of heroic dimensions, with the victor clearly identified—Man against Nature, or Man against Indian (who symbolizes Nature, not another man)—and no hint of pain or suffering may be permitted.

The preferred drawing-room artifacts, for those who could afford them, were the majestic, vaporous mountain landscapes of Moran, the bucolic fields of Durand, or the luminous seascapes of Heade. For those who could not afford the paintings, there were the imitations thereof offered by the pictorialist photographers.

It was in this artistic milieu that Vroman set out, in 1895, to become a photographer.

Middle-class, comfortable, the owner of a prosperous business, he was not a man likely to feel any deep malaise, exhibit any soul-gripping concerns, or show any inclination to ruffle the calm waters of his condition. If anyone had ample grounds to share in the complacency and optimism of the period, it was Adam Clark Vroman, in Pasadena, California, in the year 1895.

Vroman, in white shirt, at work as recorded in a film clip from one of the earliest Thomas A. Edison commercially released films. 1898 Oraibi.

Thus it is fitting that we find him, on New Year's Day of that year, ready with his new view camera to photograph the Tournament of Roses Parade on South Orange Grove Avenue in Pasadena, the local burghers of the Valley Hunt Club, decked out as Pickwickians, riding by in wagon and team, resplendent among fragrant flowers.

Later that year he wandered through the fields of Altadena, up the peaks and into the canyons of the San Gabriels, ever turning his camera on the pastoral scene, the tamed nature of Wordsworth. The only unexpected thing about the photographs made on these occasions is their fidelity to the aesthetic of straight photography. It wasn't until many years later that Alfred Stieglitz was to effect a revolution against pictorialism and establish the artistic validation of the straight image. Yet Vroman was obviously committed to using this style, the style of the "informationalists" (to coin an expression), in the service of a vision that could have had only one intent: the recording of something of beauty. The expected qualities, however, are there: the images are comfortable, guaranteed to please, the expected product of the respectable gentleman-photographer of his day.

Vroman's encounter with Helen Hunt Jackson's book *Ramona* evidently marked a turning point in his life. He was obviously deeply moved by it, and in 1895 he began a series of photographs of the *Ramona* scenes, which in 1913 came to be used in an illustrated reissue of the book. His interest in the Indians had begun, and a new outlook that was to affect his life from that time onward gradually took hold.

The dramatic moment of a new vision, however, seems to have occurred in the summer of 1895, when he first witnessed the celebrated Hopi snake dance. The diary and the photographs made on this first visit among the Indians give us considerable insight into Vroman's attitudes. He went there with great anticipation, but hardly for what seems to have happened.

To begin with, he was the typical tourist. In the diary he praises or grumbles about the food and the accommodations, describes the vicissitudes of the trip into the remote Hopi villages, notes in spare language the architecture of the villages and surrounding landscape. He comments a little on the "natives," whom he found polite and cooperative toward his photographic efforts.

His first photographs made on this trip are foursquare, dead-centered compositions of mountains, rooted as if at the very center of the earth, there to stay forever—images that convey, somewhat obviously, permanence and durability. Movement is to be found only in the turbulence of a clouded sky.

Later, in the village of Walpi, we are given scenes of the village itself and some rather timidly organized groups of natives who consented to pose for him. These are tourist views a bit above the ordinary for their superb understanding and management of the technical means, yet they are static, quiet, and curiously unmoving.

But we need to establish the scene. Here is Vroman, four days out of the city, with his party all clad in chapeaux and business suits, with neckties and garters on sleeves. They stroll with impressive incongruity along the dusty paths and streets amid ragged dogs, naked children, and burros. Here and there is a leathery old man got up in a tattered union suit, leather pants, and silver concha belt. From behind the dusky windows the shy women peep out at the strangers and giggle. How fantastically exotic, how remote from the trim lawns and durable Victorian mansions of South Orange Grove Avenue! Vroman says in his journal that it was hard for him to believe he was in America.

How does the respectable businessman from Pasadena respond to this kaleidoscope? In part he is simply overwhelmed, knowing neither where nor how to begin something he feels strangely compelled to do. For already some kind of excitement, an enriched ambience in the surroundings, is provoking him, and the conventions of his way of viewing are becoming exposed in their inadequacy.

So he does the more-or-less obvious thing to break the ice: he gets his party outdoors and makes a picture of them all standing in front of the picturesque adobe where they'd spent the night. Some of the locals are attracted to the goings-on and welcome this opportunity to look over the visitors. Soon all are back inside and Vroman gets another view, this time with natives, as they sit around drinking coffee.

More confident, he goes again into the street. Soon he takes one exposure after another: streets and houses, onto the roofs, down the trails, into the plaza where preparations for the great dance are under way. The children follow, ever curious and ever ready for a handout of pennies or candy, and they line up to have their pictures taken. So goes the morning, overwhelming Vroman with opportunities for new imagery. So vast are the possibilities that only the surface is touched.

The real dimensions of place and people somehow evade the conventional vision that made the sylvan fields of Altadena such pliant subject matter. A distressing turbulence underlies the entire scene, refusing to yield to the practiced approach. New challenges are surfacing; entirely new meanings are concealed behind the surface and demand revelation.

Finally in the afternoon the snake dance began, a totally overpowering experience that called forth every last bit of Vroman's resources, as photographer and human being. On the one hand it required complete attention to the proceedings—the profound symbolism of the action, the chanting, the costumes—and on the other hand there was the photographic business—depth-of-field considerations, stopping movement of the dancers, getting adequate exposure in the rapidly waning light, the constant changing of plate holders.

When it was all over, a hush settled upon the crowd of watchers. Vroman and his friends stood in a little group and tried to understand what had happened. It appears that for Vroman this was a turning point in his life. Perhaps for the first time in his existence the great unfathomable depths of being opened before him and he touched primordial forces deep within himself. In the presence of the sacred ceremony with the snakes, the secure little world back in Pasadena diminished to total meaninglessness.

With his characteristic gift for understatement, Vroman wrote in his diary that he had to see the snake dance again two years hence, for he had been deeply moved by its sincerity and devout spirit. He wished that others could experience it too. And, more significantly, he expressed a longing to be initiated into the snake society so that he might participate in the ceremony for the full nine days.

As it developed Vroman did return in 1897 and for the next several years to see the snake ceremony. In the ten-year period of his visits to Hopi country he managed to attend all but two of these observances. For Vroman the snake ceremony was central to the Indian religions of the Southwest, and we have reason to believe it occupied a crucial position in his personal philosophy.

If we can assume that in the awed hush on the edge of the Walpi mesa Vroman had a religious experience, we

Vroman's apartment in Pasadena, California. Approximately 1902.

may be close to understanding the growth at this time of a commitment that was to infuse his art for the next ten years. Returning to Pasadena, he devoted himself to the study of the Indians, trying to understand the complexities and difficulties in the relationship of the Indians and the whites. Somewhere in this process he determined that he could bring his skills as a photographer to the aid of the Indians. Through the photographs he could present Indian life to the whites, establish respect for their religious life, their art, their precious relationship with the land, and at the same time he would be enriching the lives of his white neighbors.

The details of working through this commitment are evident from his articles and lecture notes, as well as from the photographs themselves. He had few, if any, precedents that could have helped him in shaping this project. The use of photography to express social concern began as early as the 1870s in Europe in the work of Thomas Annan. In America in the 1880s Jacob Riis used photography in his efforts to ameliorate conditions in the New York slums. It is highly unlikely that Vroman was aware of these efforts. Photojournalism was in its infancy, and the mass media had hardly begun to circulate photographic images. The only photographs that secured fairly wide distribution were the tourist "views" and the pictures that appeared in the several photographic magazines, these being pretentious and self-indulgent and in no way manifesting social concern.

Very much on his own, therefore, Vroman set his course. It would include mainly lectures illustrated with lantern slides; he would submit articles to the photographic magazines; he would reach the gentry with a deck of playing cards showing his Indian photographs and accompanied by an explanatory leaflet; and he would lead tours to the Indian country so that people could experience for themselves something of the Indian way of life. He began to buy from the Indians the finest they had to offer in arts and crafts, and over the years was to acquire one of the most important private collections in the country of Navajo blankets, kachina dolls, pottery, and baskets. And, perhaps most important of all, he would nourish those friendships already begun in 1895 among some of the families at Walpi and later among other villages in all the pueblos. Where he could do so discreetly, he would apply some of his rapidly accumulating personal fortune to offset many of the worst conditions of poverty into which these people had been forced.

The straight photographic approach, producing full-scale, bright, sharp images, was the obvious and superb medium for the conveyance of information, and it is no surprise that it was Vroman's choice to portray Indian life. The industrious application of a technique he had already mastered could have served to transmit information, but Vroman's commitment demanded more than that. He sought to develop sympathy. The rapport he enjoyed with the Indians needed to be transferred to his audience so that they might share in the experience. For this he had to penetrate beyond the surfaces of his subjects, and through sensitive and imaginative use of his technique create pictures that would offer extensions of their personalities, provide a means whereby the viewers could realize the deeper, more intimate nature of the people he would photograph.

It must have become plain to Vroman that the static and placid approach to imagery that served him in making his earlier landscape studies was insufficient for the more human and social purposes he wished to serve. He could no longer concern himself with image-making that satisfied the conceits of a complacent society, for a new urgency was upon him and it had to find expression in his pictures.

Beginning in 1897, we see a new style begin to emerge: more vigorous and tension-filled, with Vroman exhibiting a deeper insight into his subject matter. The static compositions give way increasingly to those that force the eye out of circular pleasantries, drawing attention to significant content and demanding more participation on the part of the viewer. We find Vroman making deliberate experiments with unbalanced, dynamic arrangements of his subject matter, struggling to enhance the emotional impact of content through the use of composition. The camera is elevated in its role from an instrument that merely records into one that confronts, that in itself provokes meaningful revelations from those who sit before it.

It is in the portraits especially that Vroman's genius is most openly displayed, and through them we reach the very heart of his message. Witness the many straight-on, three-quarters studies, each rooted in the frame of the picture like a giant pyramid. The inference is immediate: here is a people strong, vigorous, proud, eternal. More mysteriously, here are people who are knowable to us . . . perhaps we have always known them! Our response arises from our own deepest natures as we gaze upon these reflections of a people still in reverent communion with the earth. We discover that their humanity is, after all, our own. They are the dwellers at the source from which we all came and to which we all shall one day return. The identity is complete.

After 1904 Vroman gave up photography among the Indians. He had successfully completed the task he had set for himself. In the remaining years of his life he continued to lecture, show his Indian photographs, and travel widely about the world. As far as we know he never returned to see his friends in the pueblos, though there was no abatement of his sympathy and concern. More than likely he was deeply discouraged by the failures of his generation to respond generously, or even humanly, to the dreadful genocide that was being consciously promoted by the Government against the Indians. Each visit to the pueblos had no doubt become more painful, as pueblo after pueblo became divided within itself, and friend betrayed friend. By 1906 open hostilities had divided the village of Oraibi. For Vroman this may well have marked the end.

Without the energy flowing from commitment, Vroman's photography after 1904 lost its power and significance. He gave up the view camera, adopted simpler roll-film cameras, and settled for making uninspired tourist pictures of his travels. Only an occasional image among these reminds us of the power of his visualization as we saw it in the Indian work.

Printing his early work occupied much of Vroman's time during his last years. He passed his prints out generously to his many friends. Across one of them he wrote "Just an amateur!" It was a characteristic expression of his deep humility, but if we look to the primary meaning of that word we discover it to be perhaps the truest description of Adam Clark Vroman.

2 | THE PHOTOGRAPHS

THE HOPIS

THE HOPI people occupy three long mesas and surrounding lands in the northeastern part of what the white man chooses to call the State of Arizona. This is an arid land, high plateau country with mild summers and cold winters. There is little rain to support a scrubby growth of sagebrush and the short piñons and junipers. Most of this rain comes in violent cloudbursts during the summer months and often does severe damage through washouts and erosion. A light veil of snow often covers the land in the winter.

But it was not always such a forbidding landscape. The Hopis trace their origins back to the time when the dwellers of the underworld emerged through an opening located somewhere near the head of Grand Canyon, where the Little Colorado River joins the Colorado River. At the time of the emergence the grass grew tall and thick across the wide plains. Rain came often and nourished abundant crops of squash, beans, maize, and melons, and wild game flourished everywhere. The Hopis were well-nourished and happy, living in the grace of those colorful, loving, and generous kachinas and spirits of the underworld.

Peace reigned over their lands because the Hopis had observed faithfully the ancient tribal customs, the ritual dances that celebrated the great gift of life, and because the Hopis kept reverence and love of their fellow men always close to their hearts. Their very name Hopi meant "people of peace."

At the time they emerged from the underworld the Hopis were given some stone tablets, which defined the boundaries of the lands they were to occupy and which they were obligated to protect. They were given two commandments—one: remember the Great Spirit and look to

Him as the Supreme Executive of this land and the Governor of this life, and two: do not destroy life, but rather encourage it.

Thus the Hopis lived a life in uncommon harmony with a universe of love, beauty, and abundance . . . until the Navajos and the white man began to encroach upon their lands.

At first, accommodation seemed possible with the invaders. There was, after all, an abundance that might be shared. The Hopis were hospitable and generous. Their prophecies had told of the coming of a True White Brother, and for a while they believed that the Spaniards might be He. They even endured uncomplainingly the Spanish name for them—Moqui—which meant "dead." They endured for a while the attempt to make them into Christians. But when the invaders tried to force them to give up their own form of worship they rebelled, and ultimately the Spanish were expelled. Although they came back to the pueblos to the east, the Spanish never returned to Hopi country in any consequential way.

But real trouble began when the whites forced the Navajos out of the valley of the Rio Grande onto the plateau to the west, the ancestral home of the Hopis. The largesse was simply not enough for all . . . and the Hopis were forced into poverty.

Without any treaty to support their claim, the white Americans then moved onto the Hopi lands, in effect confiscating them and violating all the sacred boundaries observed by the Hopis. To make the subduing of a people now grown rebellious somewhat easier, another endeavor was made to introduce Christianity, and new attempts to stamp out the native religion went hand in hand with the effort to convert. "Government" was introduced to a tribe that had done very well without government for generations, and with this government came dissension among the people. The amazing unity of the old tribal community began to distintegrate.

Today the Hopis are a people torn with internal conflicts, crowded into a land no longer capable of supporting them. Yet they are struggling, even with renewed energy, to keep their ancient traditions alive and to observe the decent and dignified imperatives of a way of life that might well form a model for the rest of the world if it were only given a chance to continue to grow from its own roots and not according to the dictates of an alien culture.

1. *Wagon train on the trail to Hopi villages. 1901.*
On his first visit to Hopi country in 1895, Vroman's party traveled in a single large lumber-wagon drawn by a pair of heavy draft horses. Later trips, such as that sponsored by the Museum-Gates Expedition in 1901, were made in the comparatively luxurious equipment shown in this photograph. The roads, however, were anything but luxurious—nothing more than a couple of dusty ruts that led across scores of miles of desolate plains, through quicksands, and over rocky embankments. The logistics of getting there were difficult enough, but the management of large camera equipment and the many glass plates and other gear that had to be carried along through all these complications stirs deep admiration for the men who accomplished these early trips, an admiration that grows as we contemplate the immense photographic achievement that resulted.

2. *"Our Home on the Mesa." 1895.*
Vroman made his first trip to Hopi country in August, 1895. Mr. H. N. Rust of South Pasadena had invited Vroman to join a party that would journey to the remote Hopi villages in time to see the legendary snake dance. The party included a Mr. Crandall and a Mrs. Lowe, the wife of Professor Lowe of Pasadena. All were to be guests of Captain Thomas V. Keam, who resided near the Hopi villages in what has become known as Keam's

Canyon. Vroman did not actually meet Captain Keam on this occasion, as the captain was in England at the time and had arranged for Mr. Godfrey Sykes to entertain the guests.

After a long and dusty trip across the desert, the party arrived the evening of August 17 and went directly to a house engaged for them by Captain Keam at Sichimovi village on First Mesa. Vroman's 1895 notebook relates the somewhat harrowing experience of getting Mrs. Lowe to the top of the mesa. The lady weighed 260 pounds and had to be carried up on a litter over a rough and rocky trail after sunset as light was failing rapidly.

This photograph was made the morning after the arrival of the party and shows, left to right, Mrs. Lowe, Mr. Crandall, Mr. Rust, Vroman, and Selledon Montoya, the team driver who brought the group from Holbrook.

Later this same morning Vroman made some twenty exposures around the village before becoming involved in photographing the snake dance.

3. *"Interior of Our House on the Mesa." 1895.*
This photograph was made August 18, the first morning Vroman spent in the Hopi villages. Mrs. Lowe is collapsed, with her fan, at the end of the room. Several villagers have dropped in to get acquainted.

4. *Trail to Walpi. 1901.*
Walpi is perhaps the most spectacular of the Pueblo locations, a long finger of flat mesa surrounded by abrupt cliffs having only a few passages across them. This was the main access trail to Walpi. Up and down this defile moved the population of the village, the men often going several miles to the fields they tended and the women going down to the springs at the base of the cliffs to get water, which they would carry back to the village in large ollas strapped to their backs.

5. *Walpi village from the northeast. 1895.*

6. *Edge of the cliff. Walpi, 1897.*
Sanitation in these mesa-top villages was achieved by throwing all refuse over the cliff. In the early days, when everything was bio-degradable, this practice created no nuisance. The white man's introduction of bottles, cans, and plastics would make this same view, if photographed today, significantly less attractive.

7. *Walpi, from the south. 1901.*

This view of Walpi was one that Vroman repeated each year he visited the pueblo. Vroman was deeply interested in the detailed changes that occurred from year to year and noted these both in his journal and in his photographic documentation. Negatives taken in earlier years from this same point of view reveal many changes, some subtle and minute, others conspicuous. Compare this photograph with the next, taken in 1897, and note how sometime between the two pictures the second story of the house in the left foreground has disappeared. Also, note the new white plaster coating on the houses in the center of the picture. The suite of photographs between these two indicates that the plastering was a slow process, going on more or less all the time during the interval, a little bit added each year.

Just below the white house is the plaza where the snake dance is held, and at the south end of the plaza stands the spectacular Sacred Rock, which figures prominently in many of the views of the Walpi snake dance.

Note also the covered passageway toward the right foreground, and the entrance to the underground ceremonial chamber, the kiva, in the right foreground.

8. *Walpi, from the south. 1897.*

9. *"A Bit of Walpi Pueblo from the South." 1895.*
This view is taken from a lower elevation than the two previous views, and the second story of the house is still present and evidently in use. The kiva entrance at the extreme left has a sign on it, evidently made from a discarded photographic mount! which can be read on the original print. Its neatly executed lettering reads: "Monkhiva, headquarters of the Antelope Society. Please don't attempt to enter. Wiki, high priest."

This was an injunction Vroman always respected. Many other photographers of the period ignored this wish of the people to carry on their ceremonies in private and to keep their sacred objects out of the sight of uninitiated eyes. It was a shameful performance, which Vroman deeply deplored, as these photographers would burst into a kiva, set up their tripods over the protests of the celebrants, and then explode a tray of flash powder. These outrages finally led the Hopi to forbid all photography of any of their ceremonies, a prohibition that holds to this day.

10. *View of Walpi from the northwest. ca. 1900.*
Reproduced from an original Vroman platinum print.

11. *"Moqui Girls and Men." 1895.*

This photograph was made the morning of August 18 and is one of the first exposures Vroman made of the residents of a Hopi village. He quickly learned how to win the confidence of the people and describes his method in his diary: "There seemed no end of subjects, and the natives were soon won over to allow us to make photos and all very cordial to us. One of the best ways of ingratiating one's self to their confidence, I found, was first to always sit down and try to explain the camera to them, then stand it up and look through it, pointed away from them, and have them look through and see [the] picture in the ground glass and, after all had seen, go out and let them see me standing on my head. It was amusing to see their surprise when [they] would put the focusing cloth back and see I was not on my head. They would look again and then come out and smile and call others to look and then they would smile too. Mothers, babies, all had to go through it, and after I had shown them all I could they never refused to allow me to make pictures of them. Only thing was they would not keep still, always forget, just at the proper time."

12. *"Moqui Children and Young Mother Carrying Child." Mishongnovi, 1898.*

Considering when it was made, and with what equipment, this is an extraordinary photograph. We are accustomed in our time to seeing captured moments, the subjects unaware they are being photographed. This is the special province of the hand-held 35-mm. camera, loaded with fast film. But this example, done with a 5″ x 7″ plate camera on a tripod, nearly defies comprehension. Here is an unposed, entirely natural, "slice of life" photograph with a rich counterpoint of curiosity, fun, and sympathy in the faces. Such a photograph is a fine accomplishment under the best of circumstances; in 1898 it was almost without precedent.

13. *A young mother and child. Mishongnovi, 1897.*

This photograph was made on Vroman's first trip to Second Mesa in Hopi country.

14. *Hopi mother and four children. Undated.*

15. *"Mid-day Meal." 1901.*

Another unposed, "candid" photograph, so astonishing an accomplishment with a 6½″ x 8½″ plate camera!

16. *Hopi girl, standing. ca. 1895.*

The squash-blossom hairstyle signifies maidenhood to the Hopis. Vroman's photographs indicate very widespread use of this hairstyle at the turn of the century. It is seen today only rarely, on special occasions.

The garment consists of a large rectangular piece of cloth woven of black wool and joined in a seam along the edges. It hangs from the right shoulder, leaving the left shoulder and arm bare. A colorfully decorated sash is wrapped around the waist, and a second cloth, with corners tied together, is draped over the shoulders. Feet are usually bare. The necklace is of shell and turquoise beads, very likely acquired through trade with the Zuñis.

These homespun fabrics gradually were replaced by cheap factory-made prints during the years Vroman photographed among the Hopi. Hopi men continue to weave these women's dress goods even today, but they are rarely worn except on ceremonial occasions.

17. *Hopi maiden. 1901.*

The magnificent jewelry is probably of Zuñi origin. The earrings are made of turquoise inlays.

18. *Oraibi mother with baby in cradleboard, woven plaques hanging about. ca. 1900.*

Reproduced from original platinotype by Vroman.

19. *Two Hopi maidens in doorway. 1901.*

The white man's commercial fabrics had been established within about five years from the time that Vroman made his first photographs of Hopi girls. Hopi men had much earlier adopted white men's clothing except for ceremonial occasions, though the soft buckskin moccasins were still preferred, as they are even today.

20. *Portrait of Supela, a snake priest from Walpi. 1900.*

21. *Naquistewa, a man of Oraibi. 1901.*

22. *Portrait of Ongha's wife. Hano village, 1901.*

The hairstyle identifies the married status.

23. *Sikutsi, young girl of Hopi. ca. 1901.*

24. *"Hopi Madonna, Silas' Wife." 1901.*

This is one of several "madonnas" that Vroman made whenever the opportunity arose. The woven plaques, introduced into the picture by the photographer, are made by the women in villages on Second Mesa and are used ceremonially, as for trays to hold sacred cornmeal. The Second Mesa style of plaque is made of a coil of grasses and native yucca fibers, wrapped with yucca fiber, and dyed in a variety of colors. A similar plaque, based on weaving fibers around a radial pattern of supporting stalks, is made at Oraibi. See Number 18.

26. *Shipaulovi village, as seen from Mishongnovi. 1901.*
Note the alternating horizontal beds of shale and sandstone, which form nearly level terraces. At the bases of the sandstone layers occasional springs provide the meager water for the villages.

The reasons for siting the pueblo villages on mesa tops is still not thoroughly understood.

27. *View looking over Mishongnovi, Shipaulovi in the distance. 1901.*
This view clearly illustrates the central plaza of the village and the surrounding houses. Access to upper stories was usually by means of outdoor ladders and stairways. It is in the upper stories that the people live, the lower levels being reserved mostly for storage purposes. The large stacks of juniper wood are used for fuel in space heating and cooking.

28. *House details. Mishongnovi, ca. 1897.*
In this illustration there is little evidence of the white man's influence, and we are able to see the pueblo much as it existed for centuries prior to the coming of the Spaniards. Still in use are the chimneys made from broken utility pots. Yucca baskets hold ears of corn. The handwoven blankets contain newly shorn wool, but very likely would have held bolls of native-grown cotton prior to the Spanish period. The doors of sawn timber are, of course, a modern innovation.

29. *"The Plaza, Mishongnovi, Showing Kiva Entrance." 1901.*
The kiva is the ceremonial chamber of most pueblo tribes. The Hopis place their kivas partially underground, hewn out of rock in a rectangular plan, with the entrance through the top. Each village has a number of kivas, reserved for the different fraternities. Most Hopi ceremonials have two aspects, the first being a secret activity involving prayer; making of symbolic paintings, objects of various sorts, and masks; and erecting of altars. The second aspect is a public activity, held in the plaza, of ritual dancing and music-making. The secret or private portions of the ceremonials are held in the kivas. The religious activity is largely the responsibility of the men of the community, though women participate in many aspects of the ceremonials and have some observances of their own.

From time to time the kiva may function also as a meeting place where nonreligious matters may be discussed, or the kiva may be used for weaving and spinning. Except for ceremonial occasions the kivas are sparsely furnished, all the paraphernalia being stored in the homes when not in use.

30. *"Old Man at Entrance to Kiva." Walpi, 1902.*

31. *House-building. Probably Mishongnovi, 1901.*
House-building in Hopi country is the woman's job, and women are the "owners" of the houses. The men help with the heaviest work, such as laying the roof beams. A married man lives in the house of his wife, and the property, like the clan relationships, follows a maternal succession.

32. *"Interior of Hooker's House." Sichimovi, 1902.*
Hooker was governor of Sichimovi village, and his house provided settings for a number of Vroman's most interesting portraits and genre studies.

This interior view shows some of the typical decoration of the Hopi home, notably the kachina dolls representing the masked deities that symbolize all aspects of Hopi life.

33. *"Hooker, Governor of Sichimovi." 1902.*
The First Mesa villages, being closest to United States Government headquarters at Keam's Canyon, felt the white man's influence most strongly. The Government agents found the pueblo social structure inscrutable and tried to introduce "government" to the people so that they could conduct their lives in an orderly manner. It seems to have escaped these authorities altogether that these villages had lived orderly lives for immeasurable generations without the "benefit" of any government whatsoever.

"Governors" were appointed by the white overlords and were expected to exercise an opposing influence to the consort of hereditary chiefs whose authority derived from religious tradition and who had long exercised this authority without compulsion but by force of example. So alien was this notion of a governor to the

Hopi people that eventually the function was abandoned.

In more recent years the "elected" tribal council has assumed a political role on the reservations. These councils tend to be divisive, acceptable only to a minority faction of so-called "progressives." The majority of the people have refused to participate in the electoral process by which the council is selected, and the council itself has been far more responsive to Government demands than it has responded to the desires of the people.

34. *"Hooker Standing in Front of His Home." 1902.*
The buckskin pouch is decorated with a painted eagle; in his hand Hooker holds a stone axe. The neckpiece is Navajo.

35. *Tom Polacca, man of Hano. 1901.*
In the early 1880s Polacca accompanied a delegation of Hopi personages who visited Government authorities in Washington, D.C. Polacca was the interpreter for Lololama, a leader in the "friendly" or "progressive" faction at the village of Oraibi.

36. *Portrait of Hopi man, Chara, age 85. 1901.*
The venerable gentleman holds in his hand a "paho," or prayer stick. F. W. Hodge gives an informative account of the making of these prayer sticks: "The making of prayer sticks among the Pueblos is a complicated ceremony, having a multitude of details to be observed. Cord of native cotton is used to attach the feathers, herbs, meal, etc., to the sticks, which, as a rule, are made of cottonwood shoots. The feathers are those of particular birds, and they must be perfect and come from particular parts of the plumage. The paints used must be ceremonially gathered, prepared, and applied. In paho-making even the refuse—chips of wood, ends of cord, etc.—is disposed of in a prescribed manner. Prayer sticks are often consecrated by being moistened with medicine, sprinkled with sacred meal, and fumigated with tobacco, and by other rites; and after prayers have been breathed into them they are sent out in the hands of messengers to be deposited in shrines, springs, and fields. Prayer sticks for family offerings are made on the occasion of ceremonies and are deposited also by authorized persons. Individual offerings of prayer sticks are also made.

"The sticks to which the plumes are attached indicate the gods to whom the prayers are offered, and the feathers convey to the gods the prayers which are breathed into the spiritual essence of the plumes. This conception is materialized in the 'breath feather,' generally the downy plumage of the eagle. Prayers are also breathed into sacred meal, pollen, and other objects offered.

"The idea of feeding the gods is expressed by one form of the Hopi prayer stick, the paho, 'water prayer,' to which a small packet of sacred meal is attached. The prayer stick may be regarded as a symbolic substitute for human sacrifice (J. W. Fewkes in Bureau of American Ethology, Sixteenth Annual Report, 1897, p. 297). Prayer sticks, nearly always painted green or blue, are frequently found with the dead in ancient Pueblo cemeteries, and great deposits of them occur in ceremonial caves in southern Arizona." (*Handbook of Indians of America North of Mexico.* Bureau of American Ethnology Bull. 30, vol. 2, p. 304).

37. *Hopi medicine man. Keam's Canyon, 1902.*
Vroman's camera case is doing duty as a posing bench.

38. *Hopi man with wool and spindle. 1901.*
This fellow is very likely a sheepherder and is equipped to camp out. Hopi men still spin wool and cotton with a hand spindle.

39. *Lesho trying moccasins on Vroman. 1901.*
Lesho was the husband of Nampeyo, the famous Hano potter. Some of her work can be seen on the shelves against the wall.

Over the several years that Vroman visited the Pueblo villages he kept collecting arts and crafts and gradually assembled one of the finest private collections.

40. *Hopi sash-weaver. ca. 1901.*
It is the men among the Hopi who are the spinners and weavers and who remain to this day the chief suppliers of ceremonial fabrics to the other tribes in the Southwest.

41. *Blanket-weaver. Oraibi, 1902.*
The large loom shown in this illustration would be used for making the woman's dress. The art of weaving as practiced among the Hopi was a possible basis for the development of weaving among the Navajo, though some modern scholarship questions this view. Hopis have continued to produce substantially the same fabrics with little if any evolution taking place in the designs. This is no doubt due to the ceremonial uses to which the fabrics are usually applied.

42. *"Ahbah, Kachina Blanket-Maker." Sichimovi, ca. 1902.*
These handsome textiles, greens, reds, and blacks against a white ground, are achieved by embroidery on white woven cotton and

are used exclusively in religious observances.

43. *Nampeyo coiling a pot. Hano, 1901.*

The people of Hano were one of the tribal groups to which the Hopi had given refuge in the past. Ultimately these groups have been absorbed into the Hopi society. The Hano people migrated to Hopi in the early eighteenth century from their ancestral homeland in the Upper Rio Grande, known as Tsawarii.

Nampeyo became interested in pottery when the Fewkes Expedition began turning up pot shards at the ancient and abandoned Hopi village of Sityatki. The designs on these old pots so intrigued Nampeyo that she began to make pots of her own with decorations based upon these old designs. Thus began a revival of pottery-making on First Mesa.

Pottery is made only by the women, and even today it still comes almost exclusively from First Mesa.

44. *Nampeyo, potter of Hano, with some of her wares. 1901.*

Hopi pottery is distinguished by rather thick walls of a rich, ocher-colored clay decorated with highly abstract symbols of birds, reptiles, or occasionally mammals, and with elegant geometric designs. The designs are usually painted in black and light hematite red.

45. *"Collection of Curios Belonging to Captain Thomas Keam." Keam's Canyon, 1900.*

On the left is a wall filled with *kachinatihu*, dolls that represent the kachinas, the deities of the Hopis. These bright, colorful images are carved from cottonwood and given to the children to help them become acquainted with the innumerable kachinas that populate the Hopi pantheon. The rugs on the floor are Navajo. The pottery is mostly ancient, recovered from the several ruined villages that surround the present Hopi pueblos. Notice the photographs, mostly gifts from Vroman, some of which are reproduced in this book.

Captain Keam died in 1904, and it appears that some of this collection, particularly the rugs, may have been passed on to Vroman.

46. *Volz's store. Oraibi, 1901.*

Volz was the owner of a chain of trading posts strung out between Cañon Diablo and Oraibi. On the 1898 trip Vroman engaged Volz as a guide and tour manager to conduct his party from Cañon Diablo to the Hopi villages over a route he had not previously taken. An anonymous article, possibly authored by Vroman, describes the accommodations provided by Volz: "At noon we halt for luncheon, but luncheon is too elegant a term, even lunch smacks too much of civilization; the proper word in Arizona for lunch is 'grub.' Almost everything one eats comes in a tin can or tin box: beans, milk, and meat; sardines, preserves, and jams—all are imported in hermetically sealed tins. Thus canned goods form a most important item in the commerce of the territory, where they are known by the comprehensive name 'air-tights.' We breakfast, dine, and sup on air-tights, and before every meal all hands are set to work with old knives and scissors, for the rare can-opener is usually missing and, by the time the air-tights have ceased to deserve the title, the workers have in the effort of opening them already developed appetites ravenous to such a degree that no time is wasted in vain longing for fresh fare. A heap of empty tins marks every halting place of the caravan. As the professor from Berlin remarked one day after lunch, in his staid, scientific tone, 'It is my conviction that in a future age the geologists will be confronted by a novel problem, for Arizona will be found covered with a stratum of tin as extensive as the border of the territory.'

"We spend the night at a second store belonging to our trader-guide about thirty miles from the railway. Mr. Volz controls three establishments: one at the Cañon Diablo station; another at a place called by courtesy 'the Lakes,' because of the water standing in the broad hollows that surround this eminence when it rains; and a third store within a few miles of Oraibi, the largest of the Moki villages, which is to be our headquarters when we reach the reservation. . . .

"After business hours the store becomes our dormitory; four men sleep on the counter, two under it, the rest on the floor. We each have new Navajo blankets to use for our bedding; the ladies of our party sleep in a storeroom with a hundred brilliant blankets piled under and around them. . . .

"Late in the afternoon of our second day on the desert, we come to Volz's third establishment, the business center of the Moki reservation. First we shake off the dust of our long two days' ride; then at a table on an improvised veranda we attack a few dozen tins of air-tights and drink a pail or two of coffee. The amount of coffee that one can consume in Arizona is incredible; it is poured out in bowls, served piping hot and without milk. We average two bowls at every meal and sleep like tops. Some of us sleep in tents, others in one of the shanties. We lie in blankets on the bare ground, cases of canned provisions and bales of goods piled high around us. . . ."

47. *"Lominomah, Hopi Bowman." Jettyto Spring, undated.*
Jettyto Spring is a stopping place between Holbrook and Keam's Canyon.

48–55. *Hairdressing, showing how the squash-blossom is achieved, step by step. Shungopavi, 1901.*
Year by year as he visited the Hopis, Vroman expanded his photographic documentation. The work of his first visit in 1895 is largely on the surface of things—what any tourist might have seen—although he recorded it with great skill and sensitivity. By 1901 he had moved his camera indoors and began to record the more intimate aspects of Hopi life. This series on hairdressing is typical of the kind of thoroughness with which he approached the task. Obviously a very high order of cooperation from his subjects was involved, especially since by this time photography was coming under increasing suspicion by the people.

56. *"Lesho, Cutting Mutton." Hano, 1901.*

57. *Oraibi girl with plaque. 1902.*
Reproduced from an original platinotype by Vroman.

58. *Making plaques. Shungopavi, 1901.*

59. *Two Hopi maidens, daughters of Hooker. Sichimovi, 1901.*
This photograph is one of several made during an inspired afternoon working with Hooker and his family. Vroman's environmental portraits are among the most stunning of his accomplishments, and the way in which this photograph quietly tells of the mysterious depths in the soul of a people raises it to the level of a masterpiece.

60. *Portrait of an Oraibi man. Pawiki, 1901.*

61. *Oraibi woman at window. 1902.*
In his notation on the sleeve for this negative, Vroman identifies his subject as "Juliet." The occasional literary allusions that Vroman made in titling his photographs suggests that he was not entirely immune from some of the inanities practiced by the salon photographers of the time.

62. *A group of boys. Oraibi, 1897.*
In his diary on August 21, 1897, Vroman wrote, "All about the town the preparations were being made. Little tots were being painted with a white pigment about limbs and faces and eagle feathers fastened in their hair, bright bits of color in clothing and a general dress-up occasion, for this was the day of the snake dance."

Note: The caption titles within quotation marks are those which are taken directly from the Vroman annotation on the negative sleeves or prints in the Pasadena Library collection. Other caption titles are either paraphrased from Vroman's annotations or supplied by the authors.

1

2

3

4

5

6

7

8

9

10

11

14

15

16

17

19

20

21

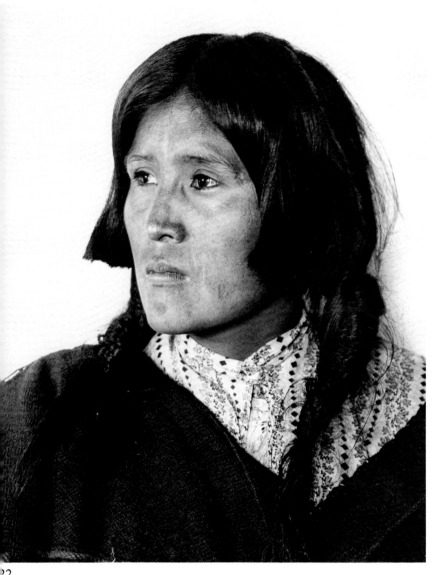

22

23

55

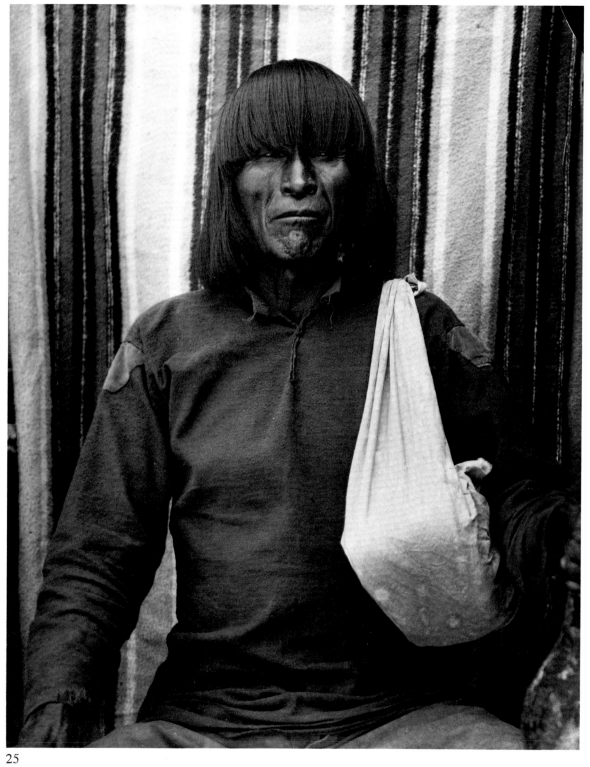

25

26

27

28

29

31

33

34

35

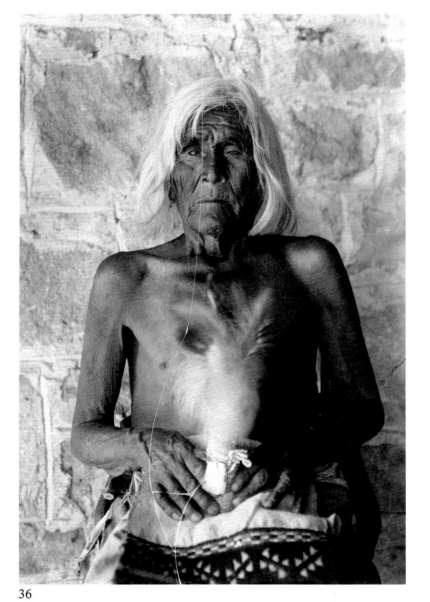

36

37

38

39

40

43

44

45

46

47

48

49

50

51

52

53

54

55

56

57

80

58

59

61

83

62

THE SNAKE CEREMONY

The photographs that follow are selected from a very large group Vroman made over the years in different villages. We have put them in an order that shows the sequential stages of the dances but have disregarded differences in location and time. Several variations in costume and in details of the performance might be noted, and the ethnologists have commented on these at length in the literature of the subject; however, the overall outlines of the ceremonies are much the same from village to village.

Photographing the snake ceremony presented a difficult technical challenge. There was severe competition among the many photographers for the best positions, and we are told of more than one ugly squabble for a piece of territory that resulted in camera stands being kicked over. The ceremony began in the late afternoon, causing severe backlighting problems and difficulty in getting depth of field and stopping motion at the same time in waning light conditions. Not infrequently equipment had to be covered up quickly against a huge downpour of rain.

On the whole, of the many photographs of the ceremony that have survived from the period, Vroman's were the most successful. Certainly his series is the most comprehensive, as he no doubt made photographs at more ceremonies than any other photographer. His group of photographs made of the 1900 Oraibi ceremony were by far his best, but the negatives from this series have evidently been lost, and we know of the images only from the platinotypes in the Pasadena Public Library.

The snake dance was first seriously studied by whites in the early 1880s, and by 1900 a great many accounts of the ceremony had appeared in print. Tourists began to witness the dance in the nineties, and Vroman reports in his 1895 notebook that, at the base of First Mesa on the evening before the dance, "we found some forty white people camped, all to see the dance. Was not a little surprised to learn there were artists of note. Authors, sculptors, newspaper correspondents from a half dozen papers, and some dozen or more ladies." By 1897 Vroman reported some two hundred whites in attendance. In addition, Navajos and other Indians would show up in large numbers to witness the dance.

In modern times the snake dance has been attended by hundreds of tourists, many brought by the busload on tours, to the maximum capacities that the villages could hold. In 1971 the ceremony at Mishongnovi was closed to all whites and any drunken Indians, the inevitable response to the sideshow atmosphere created by audiences intent only upon the sensational and with no appreciation for the devout meaning of the ritual.

Tourist attendance at the dance has always been stimulated by guidebooks and propaganda that have emphasized its bizarre features, such as the performers carrying venomous snakes in their mouths and yet mysteriously not dying on the spot of snakebite. It is significant that Vroman's accounts of the ceremony are exceptional. He remarked, even of the first dance he saw, about its awesome, devout, and reverent qualities. In his lectures and articles he frequently compared the Hopi ceremonials to Christian observances, claiming that he failed to find the latter in any way superior.

The snake ceremony is held on alternate years, with the intervening years taken up with the flute ceremony. On odd-numbered years the ceremony is held at Walpi on First Mesa and Mishongnovi on Second Mesa; on even-numbered years it was held in Oraibi, but in more recent times has been held in Hotevilla.

The exact date of the ceremony is announced eighteen days in advance of the public dance. The chief priests of the Snake and Antelope fraternities meet four days after the close of the final Niman kachina celebration to decide upon the date.

For the next eight days nothing happens; on the ninth day the Antelope and Snake men enter their respective kivas and various secret observances are made.

63. *"Snake Priest, Harry, On Way to Capture Snakes." Mishongnovi, 1901.*

This photograph was made on the tenth day after the announcement and the first day of the ceremony. This is the first day, of which there will be four, devoted to hunting for snakes. At about ten in the morning several Snake men leave the kiva equipped with digging sticks, a bag of sacred cornmeal, and a snake whip made of eagle feathers. They move to the north, capturing snakes at every opportunity for the entire day. In the evening the men return with their catch to the kiva, the bags of snakes being deposited there. The men take their evening meal in the kiva and spend the night there.

The following day an expedition heads to the west, and more snakes are gathered. By evening some large jars have been brought into the kiva and the snakes are placed in these jars.

The next day the snakes are gathered from the south, and finally, on the fourth day, they are brought in from the east. All varieties of snakes have been gathered without discrimination, up to about one half of them being rattlesnakes. Sometimes as many as eighty snakes will be caught, and a large number of jars will be required to hold them all.

64. *Kahlapti, Antelope priest. Mishongnovi, 1901.*

On the fifth day the Antelope priests are occupied in their kiva erecting an altar, a sand painting about five feet square containing rain-cloud symbols, colors to indicate the cardinal directions, and zigzag lightning symbols. Pahos are made in great numbers, and various totems and fetishes are placed about the altar. The chief Snake priest visits the Antelope kiva several times a day, where he engages in ceremonial smoking with the Antelope chief, from whom he receives pahos that he takes back to his own kiva.

As the morning star rises on the sixth day, the chief Snake priest, together with a young Snake man, enters the Antelope kiva. Also at this time the Antelope chief arrives with a young maiden. The young people are dressed in beautiful ceremonial costumes. The maiden stands at the rear of the altar, which is now surrounded by the Antelope priests, and she is given a pottery jar containing stalks of growing corn and melon vines, all of which she holds in her extended arms. Upon the open arms of the youth are laid the sacred "tiponi," a representation of a plumed serpent made of eagle feathers and endowed with great mystical power; to his hand is given a rattlesnake that has been brought over from the snake kiva.

Ancient songs are sung; holy water is sprinkled upon the sand painting; and, finally, the chief Antelope priest raises an ancient cloud-blower, lights the tobacco within it, and as the priests invoke the clouds of the four cardinal directions, he blows great clouds of smoke upon the colored sands of the painting. The ceremony concludes as the youth and maiden return the objects they have been holding.

This ceremony is repeated on the seventh day and again, this time with additional observances, on the eighth day. On this latter occasion two Snake priests, in a costume to represent the war gods, leave their kiva just before dawn and, standing on the roof near the entrance, flash a lightning shooter, a wooden frame with crossed sticks that flies out when the end sticks are pressed together—a kind of lazy tongs. This device is flashed in the four directions, one after the other, as the second priest whirls a bull-roarer about his head, simulating the sounds of thunder.

Meanwhile, the young men of the village have risen early and are making their way to the fields below the mesa, accompanied by one of the Antelope priests. About two miles from the mesa top, a shrine is reached where the priest deposits pahos and draws cloud symbols with sacred cornmeal on the ground. The men stay behind as the priest wends his way back to the mesa top, drawing four or more additional cloud symbols along the trail. When the last of these are drawn, it is a signal for the men to begin a footrace to the top of the mesa.

The race is a fantastic display of speed and endurance, uphill all the way over the steep, rocky trail. The runners, who may number in the scores, wear little bells at their knees that jingle as they run. The whole village has risen by this time and watches from the mesa edge, although at first they are barely able to make out the running figures in the dim light of dawn. The goal of the race is the top of the mesa, and the winner then goes to the roof of the Antelope kiva where he is met by the Antelope priest, who gives him his reward. This is a gourd filled with holy water, upon which has been blown consecrated smoke, and the runner takes this offering to his fields, where he deposits it. The race is the first public event of the snake ceremony.

65. *Building the kisi. Oraibi, 1898.*

While the race has been going on, the Snake men are in their kiva attending to various preparatory rites; others have gone after cottonwood boughs and some long reeds, and around noon they return with these to the central plaza. Here the green boughs and reeds are fashioned into a "kisi," a kind of enclosure capable of concealing a man along with the sacks of snakes. The kisi represents a kind of altar for both the antelope and the snake ceremonies that follow.

66. *Antelope dance. Oraibi, 1902.*

At about four in the afternoon of the eighth day the Antelope men emerge from their kiva and proceed in single file to the plaza. Their costume is a richly embroidered kilt of white cotton with a decorative border in black, red, and green. A fox skin hangs from the back of the kilt, and there is additional decoration with jewelry and body paint.

While circling the plaza four times they sprinkle sacred corn-meal, which each man carries in a gourd, at shrines near the center of the plaza. As they move about they shake rattles.

With each circuit of the plaza the file passes in front of the kisi, before which lies a rough plank covering a hole in the ground. This hole represents the entrance to the underworld and is called the "sipapu."

After the fourth circuit of the plaza the Antelopes assemble in a line in front of the kisi and the Snake men make their entrance. This illustration shows the completion of the final circuit, and the Antelopes are forming their line.

The Snake men repeat the four circuits, but their movements have a different kind of energy and their appearance borders on the fearsome, their faces blackened and daubs of white clay on their bodies. They carry in their hands snake whips made of eagle feathers.

67. *Antelope dance, Snake men lined up in front of kisi. Oraibi, 1902.*

When the Snake men have made their rounds, they line up facing the Antelopes, and both begin to sing the ancient songs to the accompaniment of the Antelope rattles and the rhythmic waving of the snake whips. Bodies sway from side to side.

When the song is completed, one of the Antelopes and one of the Snake priests go up to the kisi and remove from it a bundle of green cornstalks. Taking the bundles in his mouth, the Antelope man, accompanied by a second man who places his right arm over the left shoulder of the first, dances back and forth between the line of priests. Once more the plaza is circled, and the dance is then concluded, the participants returning to their respective kivas.

On the ninth day, the day of the final public performance, the snake dance, the same dawn ritual of the eighth day is repeated: the invocation of lightning and thunder, the traditional songs, and the footrace. And the Antelopes are in their kiva making more pahos.

In the Snake kiva the mysterious ritual of washing the snakes is commenced, and when that is completed the priests begin the preparations for the dance, getting their costumes together and applying paint to their bodies. Finally they gather the snakes together and dump them into bags, which are ultimately installed inside the kisi. By late afternoon all the preparations have been completed and the dance begins.

68. *Snake dance audience. Oraibi, 1902.*

Spectators to the dance come from far and wide: Hopis from the other villages, Navajos, visitors from other pueblos, whites. In 1902 Oraibi was even less easily visited than Walpi, and the crowds there tended to be smaller and mostly Indian.

69. *Antelope men preparing to enter the plaza. Mishongnovi, 1901.*

The Antelopes are attired much the same as they were for the antelope dance of the day before, with the additions, however, of bold zigzag stripes of lightning on their bodies, a thin line across the mouth running from ear to ear, and a brilliant headdress made of macaw feathers, with jewelry about the neck.

As they did in the antelope dance, the Antelopes circle the plaza, stamping on the sipapu and finally lining up in front of the kisi.

In his diary Vroman describes the entrance of the Antelopes at Walpi in 1895: "At last all excitement now, for in comes Wiki, the head priest of the Antelopes, a fine-featured fellow probably sixty years at least, carrying a basket of sacred meal which he sprinkles as he marches four times around the plaza followed by the other Antelopes. At the rear is one of the priests with a 'whizzer,' a flat stick some eight or ten inches long attached to a string. This he whirls around, making a noise very much like wind and lightning during a heavy thunderstorm, and no doubt this is the intention. At the fourth time around all line up at the kisi, or altar of cottonwood boughs, facing the plaza."

70. *Antelopes in line awaiting the arrival of Snake priests. Oraibi, 1900.*

The entry of the Snake priests is a moment of immense drama. The Antelopes have returned to their formation and the chanting reduces to a soft pianissimo. Then the Snake men enter at a kind of trot, fantastically made up, and the whole mood instantly changes.

This photograph was made just before the entrance of the Snakes, with the Antelopes composing themselves in their line. This is one of the few photographs of the 1900 series available for reproduction. The superior photographic quality, the sharpness, and the good lighting make this 1900 group the best that Vroman accomplished, and it is much to be regretted that the negatives are evidently lost and very few prints remain. Reproduced from a platinotype.

64

91

68

69

70

74

75

76

79

80

102

THE FLUTE CEREMONY

On those alternate years when the snake ceremony is *not* being held, the villages observe the flute ceremony. In many curious ways the flute ceremony parallels the snake, though it is regarded by Hopis as having even greater sacredness. Two societies participate, the Blue Flute and the Drab Flute.

Whites, including anthropologists, long have been satisfied that most of the Pueblo ceremonies are conducted in order to produce rain, through propitiation of the appropriate deities. Such a view misses the main point. Recent and more sensitive thinkers have penetrated deeper and discovered in these so-called "primitive" expressions a celebration of far more profound implications.

Vroman may have been among the earliest to sense the broader dimensions of Indian ceremonials. His notebooks and articles hint strongly that the mere production of rain did not suffice to explain the involved symbolism and ritual. In our own time, Laura Thompson, John Collier, and Frank Waters have tried to illuminate the deeper meaning of these ceremonials. In his book *On the Gleaming Way* (Chicago: Swallow Books, 1949) Collier says, "The experiencer knows what an experience is, and he alone; and the Pueblo Indian experiencer of the sacred drama knows that he is raised into vastness, made free from personal trouble, flooded with impersonal joy and ardor, and plunged into the ever-flowing tide of the tribal and world soul."

The flute ceremony parallels some of the sequences of the snake ceremony. There are eight days of secret observances prior to the public ceremony, but much less is known about these private rites than is known about the snake ceremony. The public portion of the ritual is given on the ninth and concluding day of the ceremony, in late August.

Our illustrations, made from the Mishongnovi ceremony of 1902, are from a second series made by Vroman of the flute ceremony at Mishongnovi. The 1900 group, known only from the platinotypes in the Pasadena Public Library collection, was superior in many respects in that it showed much closer views and had better lighting. The 1902 group was made difficult by the fact that it began to rain at the very beginning of the ceremony and continued through the end. Vroman also photographed the Oraibi ceremony, probably in 1901, and while this group of negatives has become in part scattered, and those still available have de-

teriorated badly, it is useful in showing the great difference in costumes between the two villages.

81. *"Flute Ceremony, Mishongnovi, at the Spring." 1902.*
The public portion of the flute ceremony begins at a sacred spring below the mesa. In this photograph several of the Flute men are seen sitting at the edge of the spring, feet in the water, while a priest is searching the bottom of the spring for three pottery jars, each containing a sacred fetish. During this time the ceremony at Mishongnovi was accompanied by soft chanting from the row of Flute men. On the terrace above the spring is a kind of tripod with an adornment of eagle feathers, the standard of the Flute societies.

In the Oraibi ceremony there was no chanting, but instead the priests played upon reed flutes.

82. *Leaving the spring. Mishongnovi, 1902.*
After the rites at the spring, the participants move to the terraces above and there get into their costumes. At Mishongnovi the costume consisted of a white woven cotton blanket with embroidered black borders.

83. *Flute ceremony. Oraibi, ca. 1901.*
At the same stage shown in the previous photograph, the Oraibi men wear the decorated kilts of white woven cotton, with borders of black, green, and red, a foxtail suspended at the back. Over this is placed a shield that represents the sun. This handsome piece is made of buckskin, stretched over a hoop and painted in brilliant colors. The border of the shield is of eagle feathers and dyed horsehair. The same shield is also used in the Soyal ceremony.

84. *Leaving the spring and making cloud symbols. Mishongnovi, 1902.*
Amidst gentle chanting, cloud symbols are drawn on the ground with sacred cornmeal by one of the priests. This is repeated three times as the group winds its way back to the mesa top. The two maidens and the youth represent ancestral heroes of the Flute societies, and their costuming requires exceptional attention to correctness in all details.

85. *Making cloud symbols. Mishongnovi, 1902.*
Note the very few white spectators. The flute ceremony, lacking any features that could be thought sensational, never attracted the crowds that were drawn to the snake ceremony. A few years after Vroman's time the flute ceremony was abandoned, and only in

recent times has it been revived.

86. *Going up the stair trail. Mishongnovi, 1902.*

87. *Entering the plaza. Mishongnovi, 1902.*
Three series of cloud symbols are again drawn in the plaza, and into each of these drawings one of the Flute maidens throws a doughnut-shaped offering made of reeds wrapped with grasses.

88. *In the plaza. Mishongnovi, 1902.*
Two separate groups are seen in this photograph, one is the Blue Flute clan and the other the Drab Flute clan.

89. *Chanting at the kisi. Mishongnovi, 1902.*
This is the final stage of the flute ceremony.

90. *The Blue Flute altar. Mishongnovi, 1902.*
Despite the great sacredness of the flute ceremony and the secrecy of most of its observances, Vroman was able to make this photograph of the Flute altar without any protest on the part of the priests. He writes in *Photo-Era,* "No objection was made to our entering while the making of pahos and other preliminaries were in progress." In another view of the same altar, one of the priests permitted himself to be included in the photograph. Earle Forrest, in 1908, was invited into the house (Flute altars are not set up in kivas, but in regular houses), permitted to observe much of the ceremony, and was given permission to photograph the altar.

Hopi religion contains a fundamental ethic of the brotherhood of man with all living creatures, and even (more difficult to observe!) brotherhood among all *men.* Exclusiveness in ceremonial observances somehow seems inconsistent with this ethic; yet with the immense complication of much of the ceremony it is improbable that anyone outside of the initiates themselves would have much understanding of the meaning. The feeling that those who did not understand would look on in mockery might certainly be a factor keeping the uninitiated out of certain observances. But perhaps a much stronger factor was the fear that the ceremonies would be suppressed if too much were known about them—a very serious threat around the turn of the century—and this kept the Hopis secretive about their religious life.

81

82

83

84

85

86

87

88

89

90

KACHINA DANCES

The kachina ceremonies occupy the religious calendar of the Hopis from midwinter to midsummer and thus are a far more continuous and pervasive activity than the snake and flute ceremonies, which occupy a relatively brief period in the summer. Every member of the Hopi communities is initiated into one or another of the kachina societies, and all participate in the rituals in one way or another. It is believed that the kachinas, the masked deities who represent the many forces in Hopi life, reside in the San Francisco Mountains during the months they are not occupied in the Hopi villages.

The first ceremony of the year is the winter solstice rite, and each month thereafter at least one kachina dance takes place until the Niman dance, or the home dance, is celebrated in mid-July, and this marks the return of the kachinas to their home in the mountains.

The kachinas are impersonated by male dancers wearing masks to represent the particular kachinas. Preparations for the dance and other observances are held in the kivas, to which are carried the special ritual paraphernalia from the homes of the chiefs, who store these objects in the interim.

Only in 1901 did Vroman arrive in the Hopi villages early enough to attend one of the Niman dances.

91. *Interior of kiva, with Sekatila, Kachina chief. 1901.*

92. *Niman dance. Shungopavi, 1901.*
The Hemis Kachina is the principal figure in the Niman dance. The Hemis mask is unusual in having a large, flat wooden tablet, on top of which are two eagle plumes, and around it are many of the downy breath feathers. The painting, done in many colors, shows several phallic symbols and a rainbow design.

The Hemis Kachina mana accompanies the Hemis Kachina. Dressed in the traditional woman's costume, the Hemis Kachina mana are seen in a parallel line in this illustration. These are male dancers, however, impersonating a female kachina.

93. *Niman dance. Shungopavi, 1901.*
In this view we see corn and melons, which are brought into the plaza just before the dance and represent the very first harvest of the year.

The elderly gentlemen, not in costume, are the chiefs of the respective kachina clans, and they help lead the line of dancers around the plaza.

THE BREAKUP OF ORAIBI

94. *Lololama, Bear Clan chief of Oraibi, with his son. ca. 1900.*
Toward the last years of Vroman's visitations among the Hopi, dissension among the people was slowly reaching a critical point. Put simply, the problem was whether or not to assimilate into the white man's culture. Tremendous pressures from the Government to force the children into boarding schools, removing them from their families and the community life and attempting to destroy the transmission from generation to generation of the religious life and the great traditions, was being felt acutely in all the villages. Many finally succumbed, and it was Lololama who led the way at the village of Oraibi.

Around Lololama grew the faction that was to become known as the "progressives," as opposed to those who wished to cling to the old Hopi way and who, because of their hostility toward any assimilation into the white world, became known as the "hostiles."

Lololama did not live long enough to see the final denouement of his idea. It was his nephew, Tewaquaptewa, who became the tragic hero of the events that developed in the years after Lololama died in 1901.

95. *Street in Oraibi. 1898.*
At the time this photograph was made Oraibi was the largest of the Hopi villages. The oldest continuously inhabited city in what is now the United States, it was the scene of the richest flowering of the Hopi culture. In many ways it was the leader among the Hopi villages, and it was here that the Government of the United States determined to move against the tribal ways of the Hopis, to break the back of the Hopi way of life. For if Oraibi could be subdued, the rest of the villages would have to fall in line.

For years the Government had successfully manipulated the small "progressive" faction among the Hopis, taking advantage of an old Hopi prophecy that told of the coming of the Bahana, the true White Brother, who would bring with him peace and abundance. The "hostile" faction, perhaps more literal in their interpretation of the prophecy, insisted the Government agents were

114

false, that the true Bahana would come from the underworld and that he and the Hopis would compare their traditions and discover in this way their true involvement with each other.

Trouble had broken out at Second Mesa when the Government attempted earlier to remove some of the youths from the kivas, where they were being initiated into the religious societies. The chiefs had resisted, there was some violence, and a division among the people arose as to how this act of the Government should have been met. The people hostile to the Government action tended to congregate at the village of Shungopavi; Shipaulovi and Mishongnovi tended more toward cooperation with the Government effort.

Then a smallpox epidemic broke out at Shungopavi and Government officials entered the village, forcibly taking all the inhabitants away in an attempt to clean up the people, destroy their old clothing, and fumigate the village. The leaders resisted and were rounded up and put in jail at Fort Defiance, where they were held some ninety days. Upon their return to Shungopavi their hostility to the white overlords was irrevocable. The two factions, "friendlies" and "hostiles," became increasingly polarized, and fights between them erupted more or less continuously.

Finally, Tawahonganiwa, the leader of the hostiles, decided to move with his people to Oraibi, where they were welcomed by Youkiuma, the Fire Clan leader at Oraibi and a confirmed hostile.

Oraibi's hostile faction was large at that time and the addition of more adherents to this cause was understandably disturbing to Tewaquoptewa, the friendly leader of the village. It is more or less traditional among Hopis that the Bear Clan chief, who was at that time Tewaquoptewa, is in charge of the secular and administrative affairs of the village. Tewaquoptewa thus undertook to have the entire hostile faction removed from the village, and he picked out a distant ruin to the north which the people could restore and use. This plan, of course, won no enthusiasm from Youkiuma or his group.

Finally, a few days after the snake ceremony in 1906, open fighting broke out. The friendlies were badly outnumbered, so Tewaquoptewa called upon the friendly factions of Second Mesa and the distant village of Moenkopi to send in reserves. For a couple of days there was much pushing and shoving as the friendlies tried unsuccessfully to evict the hostiles. Because of the very intricate clan and religious society relationships among the Hopis—the "cement" that had so effectively held these people together in a unified community across generations—this conflict was pitting mother against child, brother against brother.

To avoid possible bloodshed, the two opposing leaders finally hit upon a plan whereby the issue could be settled. One side or the other would voluntarily leave the village, depending upon the outcome of a "push-of-war," in which the men of each faction would line up on opposite sides of a line drawn on the ground and each group would try to push the leader of the opposite one across the line. Whoever got pushed over the line would lose, and would take his people and leave the village by nightfall.

There were about two hundred hostiles and one hundred friendlies engaged in the struggle, in which from time to time the frail Youkiuma would be pushed into the air. The pushing was very exhausting, and now and then both sides would agree to a rest. Finally Youkiuma was shoved over the line. He pronounced his defeat and gathered his band together to leave. Taking what provisions and household goods they could carry, they left the village in the afternoon, headed across the mesa to the west.

A few miles out they came to the site of what became known as Hotevilla, a stretch of mesa overlooking the vast empty country to the west, covered only with scattered piñon and juniper trees. Here, under the trees, the first encampment was made and work toward building a new village was begun.

There were great difficulties at first. The Government officials were very displeased by what had happened at Oraibi. Tewaquoptewa was blamed for ineptitude in permitting the withdrawal of the hostiles, in spite of his insistence that he had done what he thought to be right under the circumstances and that all had been intended as an act of friendship to the United States Government. The demand was made upon him to secure the return of the hostiles to Oraibi. An army captain was put in charge to see that this was carried out.

The captain, seeing that Youkiuma was unwilling to come back to Oraibi, planned to have Tewaquoptewa assassinate him. Soldiers and Navajo police were brought out to Hotevilla, and word was sent in to Youkiuma that he was to present himself at sunrise when he would be shot by Tewaquoptewa.

As the sun came up that morning, Youkiuma appeared at the top of a sand dune in front of the assembled troops. Tewaquoptewa was handed a gun and ordered by the captain to fire. He refused, and as Youkiuma simply stood there, a perfect target, the miserable

Tewaquoptewa had to refuse four separate orders to fire. He was finally placed under arrest, charges unspecified, and within a few days was sent to the Indian School at Riverside, California. Then the male leaders of Hotevilla were rounded up and sent to various places. Youkiuma and Tawahonganiwa were put in the penitentiary at Florence, Arizona; others in the stockade at Fort Wingate; and still others sent to the Indian School at Carlisle, Pennsylvania. The women and children were forced to build their own shelters and gather what food they could. With winter coming on they had little time to accomplish anything; yet in spite of incredible hardships and privations they managed to survive into the spring, when the men were released and the building of the village could proceed.

Youkiuma held fast to his convictions, which cost him many months in various jails around the country, including a year at Alcatraz. Increasing disillusionment with the hypocrisy and duplicity of the Government agents won new adherents to the hostile cause. Hotevilla grew and prospered over the years, and Youkiuma remained a revered leader.

The Government continued its attempts to abduct the children and pack them off to boarding school at Keam's Canyon. On one occasion they were not allowed to return for three years. When they finally did come back for a vacation, the Hotevilla people would not permit them to return to school. The villagers had become skilled at hiding the children from the agents who would come to the village to fetch them. Continual negotiations went on over this matter of school, and finally Youkiuma was taken to Washington, D.C., to talk with President Taft about the situation. Old Youkiuma remained as adamant as ever and no deal was made. When he came back and the villagers continued to resist the Government efforts, Youkiuma was once again, for the ninth time, hauled off to jail.

The question was not resolved until, in recent times, a day school was put up at the edge of the village. Children now attend the school but are able to live at home, where they can continue, as of old, to receive instruction in the great tribal traditions and can learn to take their places in the community life.

Hotevilla today, under the wise leadership of its old chiefs, represents the stronghold of the ancient Hopi way. It remains at odds with the Government, and with its instrument, the Hopi Tribal Council. It has become a kind of symbol in the modern struggle for Indian nationalism.

On the other hand, Oraibi has fallen into ruin. Its population declined over the years until it was no longer possible for the men to carry on the simplest of the ceremonies. Whole streets became empty, the dust blowing down them no longer finding footprints to fill. Rains washed into rooms no longer lived in, and the walls crumbled into mounds of dirt.

Tewaquoptewa was finally released and returned to his village, betrayed and disillusioned. He was still the Kickmongwi, the secular chief of the village, but there were fewer constituents every year. He settled into making kachina dolls, at which he became expert and famous.

In our photograph we see a street no longer there.

91

92

93

94

95

THE ZUÑIS

IN THE WINTER of 1528 an exploring party of Spanish was shipwrecked somewhere near the west coast of Florida, and, after imprisonment and hardships endured at the hands of the Indians, four survivors of this ill-fated party finally made their escape and began one of the most fascinating and indeed miraculous treks across the unknown lands north of the Gulf of Mexico. Álvar Núñez, Cabeza de Vaca, who became leader of the heroic little band, filed with the King of Spain a detailed report of his adventure after he had arrived back among his countrymen eight years later.

Núñez evidently did not see any of the pueblos of the Southwest, though he seems to have passed very near to the southernmost of them as he crossed the Rio Grande somewhere near present-day El Paso. But he had heard from the Indians many stories of magnificent jeweled cities to the north, with streets paved with gold. Núñez' reports stirred the Spanish in Mexico into further explorations of the country to the north. The first of these, under the leadership of Fray Marcos of Niza, had in its party Estavanico, a freed black slave who was one of the members of Núñez' party.

When Fray Marcos reached what is now southern Arizona, he sent Estavanico and some Sonoran Indians he had recruited into his party ahead to advise the tribes of his coming. It was Estavanico who first set European eyes on the Zuñi village of Hawikuh.

Estavanico did not live to tell of what he saw; he was killed, along with several of his companions, by the Zuñis. Word got back to Fray Marcos, who nevertheless pressed on, and from a rise at some distance he looked upon Hawikuh. He did not get into the village, but allowed his imagination to run a bit wild, and upon returning to Mexico he described a rich and prosperous nation containing seven cities, the Kingdom of Cibola.

It was Fray Marcos' exuberant descriptions that led to the formation of a new and well-outfitted expedition, with soldiers under the command of Francisco Vasquez Coronado. In 1540 the expedition set forth to conquer the fabled cities. But upon setting foot in Hawikuh, Coronado realized that the seven "cities" were only a cluster of seven closely located villages, with dust, not gold, in the streets. Fray Marcos' account suddenly and painfully was exposed as a complete fraud.

Coronado moved on, visiting Hopi and the Grand Canyon, and finally settling for the winter among the pueblos of the Rio Grande. He created trouble wherever he went, exacting tribute from the tribes and entering into skirmishes when he found them uncooperative. He had established very early the mode that was to characterize European-Indian relationships down to the present time.

The name Zuñi was conferred upon a people who called themselves the Ashiwi by Antonio de Espejo, in 1583. At this time Espejo found the villages to be reduced to six in number, in which he estimated—no doubt a wild exaggeration—some twenty thousand to be living.

By the time the Spanish were expelled from the region in 1680, the Zuñis were living in but three villages: Halona, Matsaki, and Kiakima. Hawikuh had been the scene a decade earlier of a big attack by Navajos or Apaches. Both the Christian mission established there and its resident priest were destroyed, and the villagers were scattered, never coming back to resettle the village.

When the Spanish returned in 1692, the people had concentrated themselves in the single village of Halona, the site of the present-day Zuñi community, located in a broad valley on the north bank of the Zuñi River approximately thirty-five miles south of the modern town of Gallup, New Mexico.

A new church was begun in 1692, but it was never seriously attended by the Zuñi people. From time to time the resident priest would be expelled. At other times the villagers would desert the town and move to the top of Taayalona, the Zuñi sacred mountain, in order to ward off more effectively some attacking force of Spanish or Navajos. The harassment of Zuñi went on for years, and to this day Mexicans and Navajos are made to feel unwelcome should they happen to stray into the Zuñi village.

The social and religious life of the Zuñis are rather well understood today due to the dedicated efforts of Frank Hamilton Cushing and Mathilde Cox Stevenson, two colorful anthropologists who lived among the people for several years. Both were outrageously arrogant and condescending busybodies who felt no reservations about prying into the most secret and private parts of Zuñi life. Mrs. Stevenson's accounts in particular are embarrassing to read today, as much for their unabashed confessions about how she obtained her information as for their revelation of the perverse lengths to which the pursuit of objective science can carry one. We read these papers only to discover uncomfortably that we end up knowing more than we want to know, having learned more than we had any right to learn.

The Zuñi history, like the Hopi, tells of the coming of the people from an underworld Eden. The place of emergence is remote from the present Zuñi village. The underworld gods had instructed the Ashiwi to discover the middle point, the center of the earth above, and there to establish their village.

After long years of traveling and searching, the middle point was finally found, and the Zuñi have lived there ever since. The gods had always helped them, and continue to help them, and the Ashiwi express their gratitude and reverence through the observance of a rich and colorful ceremonial calendar.

The main ceremony is a celebration of the winter solstice, the Shalako, in which a magnificent twelve-foot-high Shalako kachina appears with feather headdress, great horns, and a long clacking beak. Vroman, unfortunately, never witnessed this most important of the Zuñi rites.

96. *Looking over the roofs of Zuñi. 1897.*
In this view, looking toward the highest houses in the village, note the chimneys made of broken pots, and the *hornos*, mound-shaped ovens on the rooftops. The *hornos* were possibly introduced by the Spanish, though there is some reason to believe that the Indians themselves had invented these ovens. They are made of stones and adobe, with an opening at the top for the release of the smoke and a side opening for placing loaves in the oven. A fire of cedar wood built in the oven is allowed to burn for several hours until the walls become thoroughly heated. The ashes are then pulled out and bread is put into the oven with long-handled paddles. A great many loaves can be baked at one time, and at least two complete oven-loads will bake after a single firing. Occasionally, these ovens are used as kennels for the ubiquitous dogs that inhabit the pueblo.

97. *View of plaza. 1897.*
At the time Vroman visited Zuñi in 1897, the people were out in the fields bringing in the harvest. Only a few remained in the village, and the several photographs made at the time give the impression of the village's being deserted. In his notebook Vroman reports making twenty-five exposures in one day at Zuñi.

98. *Zuñi Pueblo, showing new construction. ca. 1899.*
This view shows the highest buildings in Zuñi, reaching five stories from the ground level. It is thought that at one time there were seven-story houses in Zuñi, which would have made Zuñi the highest and most complex of Pueblo buildings in modern times. Pueblo

architecture reached its greatest sophistication in earlier times, however, in the monumental buildings of Chaco Canyon and Mesa Verde. Present-day buildings show less imagination and skill.

As in most of the other pueblos, the women of the community take a major role in house-building, with special interest in the plastering and finishing, while the men lay the stones and heavy wooden beams.

99. *Zuñi interior. 1897.*

100. *Interior, room used for ceremonial purposes. 1899.*
The Zuñis generally used specially designated rooms of ordinary houses for their ceremonial observances. These rooms extend east and west in order that the altar may face the East and be struck by the first light of day as it comes through a window at the east end of the room.

Since the rooms are used most of the year as ordinary living rooms, the occupying family must move out temporarily at the time a ceremony is scheduled. The room is then thoroughly cleaned and is often replastered and decorated with motifs appropriate to the clans or fraternities involved in the ceremony. Upon completion of the rites, the room is returned to the family that lives in the house.

This room is decorated with symbols of the Mu-la-kwe, or Macaw clan. The tablet that hangs from the ceiling beam is a prayer offering placed there at the conclusion of the ceremony and is left in position throughout the year until it is replaced following another ceremony.

101, 102. *Two portraits of Marmon, governor of Zuñi Pueblo.*
The long hair appears in a photograph made in August, 1904; the other is either 1897 or 1899. Long hair among most of the Pueblo people signifies initiation into one or more of the religious societies and may not be worn until a man has been properly ordained. Since the long hair represents a kind of badge of religious attainment and commands a special respect on the part of the people, the United States Government found that forcing the men to cut their hair subdued and humiliated them.

Vroman was in the habit of sending money to his friends in the pueblos and usually sent this in care of the superintendent of the reservation. On at least one occasion he discovered later that the superintendent had distributed the money only to those villagers who wore short hair and thus symbolized their cooperation with the white overlords. Vroman was expectedly outraged and wrote a stinging letter to the superintendent.

103, 104, 105. *Portraits of Zuñi men.*
Vroman seems to have had a long procession of sitters for portraits on his 1899 visit to Zuñi. Earlier, in 1897, he complained in his notebook: "It was rather more difficult to have the natives pose for us. All were willing for a price, but evidently they have met more white people than the Mokis and will do nothing without pay." On his second visit in 1899, Vroman brought with him prints he had made on his first visit, and this appears to have opened the way for making a long suite of Zuñi portraits.

In one of his *Photo-Era* articles Vroman commented: "Among the people you will find many strong faces, the men especially, I think, averaging stronger in character than at any other pueblo, and one always receives a warm welcome on a second visit if he has given no cause for offense on the previous visit."

106. *Carlito, a Zuñi principale. 1899.*

107. *Zuñi man, an albino. 1899.*
Albinism is fairly common among Zuñi and Hopi. At the time Vroman was at Zuñi there were six albinos in the village, all from different families.

108. *Pahl-owat-ti-wa. 1899.*
In his lecture notes, Vroman writes that this Zuñi *principale* "stood as sponsor, or God-father to Dr. (F. W.) Hodge of Washington, when he was initiated into one of the Zuñi societies while Hodge lived at the pueblo with Frank Cushing." When Hodge visited the pueblo in 1899 with Vroman, old Pahl-owat-ti-wa rode in forty miles from his fields to the village on a burro in order to greet his old friend.

109. *Two women with ollas on their heads. 1897.*
This photograph illustrates the standard means of carrying water from the springs, or food from the fields, among the Pueblo people . . . that is, until the introduction of the galvanized pail with a handle! The tourist demand for pottery became so great that even those who made it could hardly afford to keep it.

110. *"At the Metates." 1899.*
Corn, ground to the fineness of flour, is a staple among all the pueblo tribes. The Zuñi make a festive corn wafer, called *he-we*,

similar to the Hopi piki. A thick gruel of corn flour, often colored with herbs, is swept with the hand quickly across a smooth, heated stone upon which it bakes almost instantaneously. It is then picked off the stone, rolled up, and is ready to eat.

111. *Turquoise drilling. 1899.*
Zuñi men have long done distinguished work in turquoise and shell beads, which are widely traded among the other pueblos.

112. *The rain dance. 1899.*
This ceremonial is held at frequent intervals during the summer months. Preceded by an elaborate and secret summer solstice ceremony, the rain dances are abbreviated versions of the final, and public, portions of the solstice ceremony. The principal dancers are the Korkokshi, "dancers for good."

Vroman described his 1899 visit to Zuñi in *Photo-Era*: "It so happened that we reached the pueblo on the evening of the return from the pilgrimage to the Sacred Lake, some fifty miles south of the pueblo, where they had gone the day previous to perform certain rites preparatory to the rain dance that was to take place that night and the following days. This is one of their most important ceremonies and, as there had been no rain for many weeks, it had become a serious matter with them. Hence their long pilgrimage to the Sacred Lake, which we were told only takes place in exceptionally dry seasons as a last resort, after all other prayers and petitions have failed. Surely, after seeing the earnest prayerful appeal to their divinity, as shown in their faces, one could not question their sincerity, and we followed the sixty or more gorgeously costumed dancers more with a feeling of reverence than of curiosity, as they marched into the pueblo, just as the sun dropped behind the Zuñi buttes in the west."

113. *Rain dance. 1899.*
In this enlarged portion of a rain dance negative the Korkokshi costume can be more readily examined. The bodies of the dancers are covered with pink clay, gathered at the Sacred Lake. Feathers of the macaw and eagle adorn the top of the head, both birds representing sacred principles in the Zuñi mythology. The bearded masks are made of buckskin, painted blue, and are hung with strands of braided horsehair. A girdle of spruce boughs and anklets of the same provide a rich green accent and symbolize the miracle of all living things. The kilt is woven by the Hopi and secured from them through trade. The figure dressed to represent a female deity is

actually a man, as no women perform in this dance.

114. *"Zuñi Rain Dance, With Clowns." 1899.*

Vroman, in *Photo-Era*, described the sacred clowns, the curious figures that participate in seeming incongruity in many Pueblo ceremonials: "One strange feature is the Coshira, or Mud-heads, as they are called. Ten men with canvas masks over their heads, with grotesque faces that would frighten one out of a year's growth if come upon suddenly, go through all kinds of pranks and by-play, to entertain the spectators."

The Mud-heads are among the most sacred representations of the Zuñi kachinas, wearing masks that are supposed to suggest the idiot offspring of incestuous unions. They are warnings, to all who look upon them, against evil, and especially against sexual license. During the ceremonies they carry on with outrageous and often obscene gestures, running around in the plaza and up on the roofs, a wild counterpoint to the solemnity of the sacred dances.

115. *Rain dance, final stage. 1899.*

The column of dancers here enters into a ceremonial room through the roof of one of the houses. Here the performers will remove their ceremonial attire and indulge in a feast, breaking a total fast that began the previous evening.

116. *Sacred clowns in the plaza. 1899.*

This late afternoon photograph shows the Mud-heads loafing in the plaza at the conclusion of the rain dance.

Around their necks these clowns wear a kind of scarf of black wool; otherwise their bodies are nude, painted with a reddish clay.

96

97

98

99

100

101

102

130

03

104

131

105

106

107

108

110

111

112

113

139

114

115

116

PUEBLOS OF THE RIO GRANDE

THE PUEBLOS of the Rio Grande, sometimes called the eastern pueblos, are strung like a chain of beads along the borders of the Rio Grande and its tributaries, beginning in the south with Isleta, just outside the modern city of Albuquerque, and reaching to Taos in the north. In the not too distant past a few pueblos remained south of Isleta as far as El Paso, but these were absorbed into the local Hispanic populations during the early nineteenth century.

These pueblos do not share common linguistic roots. Rather, several languages of very different grammar and vocabulary indicate that these peoples come from a variety of ancestral stocks. This fact is further borne out by the remarkable differences in religious practices and creation myths. However, in their social organization, farming practices, and architecture these people have broad similarities.

The first Spanish settlement in the area was near the present-day pueblo of San Juan, about halfway between Santa Fe and Taos. Spanish influences on pueblo life were somewhat proportional to the proximity of the pueblo towns to the seats of the Spanish colonial government, chiefly at Santa Fe. For a long period in the history of the Rio Grande pueblos, Spanish was a second language, Spanish surnames were adopted by the villagers (though they all continued to be given their own tribal names), and Christian churches were established and maintained. Further to the west, as at Zuñi and Hopi, Spanish influences were minimal by comparison.

The early Spanish conquerors were a ruthless gang who demanded heavy tribute from the pueblos and carried many of the people off into slavery, all the while attempting to Christianize them. By 1680 the pueblos had had enough of this treatment and successfully expelled the Spanish from the entire area. For twelve years the pueblos managed to keep the Spanish from their lands, and when the invaders finally returned, they were prepared to deal with the pueblos on a more restrained and humane basis.

Meanwhile, raids by the nomadic Navajos and Apaches were causing great trouble to the pueblos, and to fend off these raiders the pueblos sought the active assistance of the Spanish military. Alliances developed, and for many years there was active cooperation between pueblos and the military garrisons.

Religion continued to be a source of difficulties between the Europeans and the Indians. The first attempts to force Christianity on the pueblos included active suppression of the native religions. Later the missionaries were willing to permit the native ceremonials to be performed, trusting that the "true" faith would sooner or later prevail. The pueblo people learned to compartmentalize their religious life, giving a kind of token allegiance to Christianity on Sunday but carrying on their own religious life during the rest of the week, a practice that more or less continues to this day.

When the Anglos moved into the territory after the Mexican War, Protestantism attempted to move against both the entrenched Catholic power and the native religions, but it was not until 1900 that Protestantism achieved any results. The Indian Bureau came under strong influence from Protestant missionaries and by 1900 was able to secure an order, the Religious Crimes Code, that made it "illegal" for an Indian to participate in any ceremonial that could be considered "offensive" to Christian standards. The local Indian agents were empowered to arrest and punish any Indian who in their opinion was in violation of the code. This had the effect of driving native ceremonials "underground," into secrecy. Enforcement of this preposterous edict appears to have been most rigorous among the Rio Grande pueblos and no doubt goes far to explain the reticence on the part of many of the pueblos, such as Santo Domingo, to admit white observers to their ceremonials. The code was withdrawn in 1923, and from that time to the present there has been a steady revival of the old ceremonies, with increasing participation on the part of the villagers. Even those who have gone to live in the cities are returning increasingly at ceremonial time to assume their roles in community life.

Like the Hopis and the Zuñis, the eastern pueblos rely on farming as the basis of their economy. There is strong evidence that at the time of the first Spanish conquest the Rio Grande people were experimenting with irrigation and losing their dependence upon rainfall to water their crops. In any case, their present farming practice does make use of irrigation, and they produce some superb crops of melons, beans, corn, and fruit.

After the rough-and-ready conquistadors and their mercenaries and slaves settled down into more orderly lives on the lands around the pueblos, there was much give-and-take between the Hispanic farmers and the pueblo farmers, to the degree that intermarriage, and a kind of assimilation that worked both ways, began to take place.

When the Navajos and Apaches were finally confined to reservations and their raids against the pueblos ceased, life in the villages settled down to the form we see today. The religious problem was the last thing to quiet down, however, all sides yielding to a kind of acceptance of a status quo that left nothing decided.

In 1899, when Vroman made his tour through these pueblos, conditions were not dissimilar from those in our time. The great art of weaving had been abandoned long before, but pottery-making was enjoying a revival. The political life of the communities, something they got along without quite well before the coming of the white man, was causing friction among factions in the villages, friction usually related to how the tribe should respond to pressures or overtures from the surrounding white community. New tensions between pueblo and Hispanic communities were just beginning to surface as competition for land became more acute and as increasing numbers of Anglos were moving into the territory and showing a preferential treatment toward the pueblos to the disadvantage of the Hispanos.

117. *Laguna Pueblo, the old Spanish Church from the Southeast. 1897.*

    After his visit to Zuñi in 1897, Vroman went by rail to Laguna Pueblo, where he met Professor Frederick Webb Hodge, of the Smithsonian Institution. Hodge invited Vroman to join his party as photographer and to accompany him in the proposed ascent of Katsimo, the Enchanted Mesa, which stood a few miles to the Southwest, between Laguna and Acoma. On September 1 Vroman went out into the village early in the morning, before the party got under way, and made six exposures, of which this is one. Vroman appears to have visited Laguna only once again, in 1899.

118. *Laguna Pueblo, interior of the old Church. 1897.*

    When this photograph was made, the church was no doubt in much the same condition as it was at its founding in 1700. The wall decorations of Indian motifs—rain, thunder, clouds, the sun and moon—would very likely have been prohibited by the missionaries before the Pueblo Revolt of 1680, but in the somewhat more tolerant attitude of the reconquest, the Church permitted the blending of the native with the Christian religion. Indeed, Christianity was never able to displace the native religions of any of the pueblos. The old ceremonials and beliefs persist with the Christian observances, simply forming an additional expression of the old faiths,

rather as if Jesus had become a kachina.

    This church is an eloquent expression of how the religions exist side by side, the symbolic murals of native themes leading up to the baroque splendor of the Christian altar.

119. *Acoma Pueblo, the Camino del Padre. 1902.*

    As part of the Hodge expedition to climb Katsimo in 1897, Vroman also visited Acoma, and described in his notebook the camp at the foot of the mesa: "After supper we climbed the ladder trail we had heard so much about and spent an hour walking about the pueblo. Everything was excitement and preparations for the great La Fiesta de San Estavan which takes place tomorrow.

    "Mr. [Charles] Lummis calls Acoma the most wonderful city in America. Certainly so far as location is concerned it is . . . a great island rock with perpendicular sides 350 feet above the valley with but two accessible points, one almost a trail, almost a ladder, the other a horse trail so steep one doubts a horse ever going up it. But history tells us how Coronado's army fought [its] way up this same trail in 1540, and today Acoma stands as described in the recent translation of his historian's writing, by Winship."

120. *Acoma, House of the governor. 1897.*

    Vroman's notebook of 1897 states: "The governor of Acoma is a Jew, Solomon Bibo, who married an Acoma woman and lived here some years as a trader, but recently moved to Laguna. Appears to be a common, average fellow, nothing remarkable or even what one would consider overbright. He had supplied a small amount of fireworks and a celebration was going on as we came up. Major Pradt of Laguna was one of our party and so we had the pleasure of meeting the governor."

121. *Acoma, First Street, showing ovens. September 3, 1897.*

122. *"Acoma, View of Pueblo from Roof of the Old Church." 1904.*

    In the distance at the right is the fabled mesa, Katsimo. The story of the Hodge ascent of the mesa was told by Vroman in one of his *Photo-Era* articles.

    Conflicting theory among the archaeologists as to whether or not the old Acoma legends about their people having once lived atop Katsimo finally led a Professor Libby to attempt to climb the hitherto unclimbed rock. His method was to fire a cannonball, with rope attached, over the end of the mesa and then haul himself to the top. This was successful, except that the professor found himself on a small, isolated platform and was unable to breach a chasm that would have put him on the main part of the mesa. In any event, he concluded from this trifling examination that the legends must have been false; there was no evidence of human occupation on the mesa.

This conclusion was not accepted by Hodge, so he came in 1897 prepared to climb the main part of the mesa using a series of telescoping ladders. Going up a long talus slope and then using the ladders to get over a vertical cliff, the entire party was successful in getting on top, where they stayed overnight and where they found evidence in the form of shards and worked stone to convince them people had indeed inhabited the mesa at one time. Vroman hauled his big plate-camera to the top and made a number of exposures.

123. *"A Daughter of Acoma." 1899.*

124. *Acoma, Mary painting pottery. 1902.*
Acoma pottery vessels are among the finest in all the pueblos. The thin walls ring brightly when tapped; the forms are eloquent, the decoration powerful yet accomplished with very fine and precise brushwork. Using several simple themes, such as parallel lines to suggest rain, the women potters of the pueblos display an almost uncanny versatility. Rarely are two pots alike, and the inventiveness that goes into each design is truly awesome.

125. *Acoma, Mary with olla on her head. 1902.*
This striking lady posed for a great many environmental portraits when Vroman visited Acoma in 1902 and 1904.

126. *Acoma, firing pottery. 1904.*
Pueblo pottery is fired at the low temperatures of an open cedarwood fire. The setting for this elegant photograph is one of the pockets in the rock over the top edge of the mesa, a sheltered spot offering freedom from drafts that might interfere with a successful firing.

127. *Acoma, Mary holding olla. 1900.*
Mary's costume is as splendid as the pot she holds. The woolen overgarment is very deep blue, dyed with native indigo, while the sash, probably made by Hopi, is red with green and white accents. The leggings are white buckskin.

The weaving art has almost entirely vanished from Acoma, and most of the fabrics that were not store-bought were traded with other pueblos.

128. *"Governor of Acoma, with Homer." 1902.*
It is apparent from this photograph that the governorship changed hands at Acoma since Vroman's first visit in 1897. Homer is not further identified.

129. *"Isleta Pueblo, a Bit of the Old Church from Northeast." 1899.*
Vroman made a complete series of all the pueblo mission churches along the Rio Grande in 1899. This was a seven-week assignment he undertook at the behest of Dr. Hodge.

This building dates from 1629, and is possibly one of the oldest of the pueblo churches. However, it seems to have fallen into ruin more than once, and was evidently burned and used as a corral right after the Pueblo Revolt. It has gone through a number of reconstructions, a major one in 1881.

130. *"Woman of Isleta with Olla on Her Head." 1899.*
While making his mission series in the eastern pueblos, Vroman used the occasion to make portraits of many of the villagers, some of these of exceptional beauty and value. But, moving rapidly from one village to the next, he was not able to record very much of an in-depth view of the lives of the people.

131. *Isleta girl standing at ladder, "Reyestojila." 1902.*

132. *Isleta Pueblo, an old lady with bread, standing by an oven. 1902.*
The art of making bread is an ancient one in the pueblos. Antonio de Espejo, one of the early Spanish explorers, describes how he was met by villagers in the Rio Grande pueblos in 1582: "The inhabitants of each town came out to meet us, took us to their pueblos, and gave us quantities of turkeys, corn, beans, and tortillas, with other kinds of bread, which they make more skillfully than the Mexican people. They grind raw corn on very large stones, five or six women working together in a single mill, and from the flour they make many kinds of bread." The golden loaves in this photograph were probably made from wheat flour, which was introduced by the Anglos. The superb quality of the bread continues to this day and is eagerly sought out by residents living now in the vicinity of the pueblo villages.

133. *Girl of Isleta. 1899.*

134. *Portrait of Isleta man, Lucero. 1902.*

135. *Plaza and estufa. Cochiti Pueblo, 1899.*
The estufa is the kiva of the eastern pueblos. Used in the same way

as the kiva, the estufas are generally larger, of round rather than rectangular outline, and are situated more above the ground. These circular rooms were elaborated into ones of immense size in some of the older cities now in ruins, such as at Chaco Canyon and Aztec Ruin.

136. *Corn-dance clown. Santo Domingo Pueblo, 1899.*
Vroman was able to make a group of photographs of the corn dance at Santo Domingo. Unfortunately, the negatives of this series were lost or damaged somehow in making their way to the Los Angeles Museum collection. This is to be regretted all the more since Santo Domingo has always been a very conservative pueblo and imposed severe restrictions against photography and even entry into the village. Thus, very few photographs of this pueblo have been made at any time.

137. *Church. Santo Domingo Pueblo, 1899.*
This church was less than a decade old when this photograph was made. Today the façade is graced with a striking mural.

138. *Church. San Ildefonso Pueblo, 1899.*
Built in 1706, demolished finally in 1910, this church had long fallen into disuse at the time Vroman made his photograph.

139. *Church. Pojoaque, 1899.*
Nothing remains of this church today, nor does anything remain of the Pojoaque village. Its people have assimilated into the surrounding Hispano communities. The church dates from 1707 and was abandoned about 1915.

140. *Church. Nambe Pueblo, 1899.*
Started in 1729, abandoned in 1890, an attempt was made in the early 1900s to rehabilitate the structure. The results were a disaster aesthetically, but worse was in store. In 1909 a huge storm destroyed the building completely, its structure having been seriously damaged in the remodeling.

141. *Estufa at Nambe. 1899.*

142, 143. *José Leandro Tofoya, Governor of Santa Clara Pueblo, and Governor Tofoya with his grandchildren. 1899.*

144. *Mission. Santa Clara Pueblo, 1899.*
A superb example of Franciscan architecture in the New Mexican pueblos, Santa Clara mission was built about 1761, of cruciform

plan, about 135 feet long. An attempt in the early 1900s to modernize the building, as at Nambe, so weakened the structure that it, too, collapsed in a storm and was finally abandoned about 1918. A new church was rebuilt on the site, following loosely the plan of the original building. The modern version betrays the plastic culture of its time and lacks altogether the dignity and simplicity of the church we see in this photograph.

145. *Altar, Santa Clara mission church. 1899.*

146. *Mission church. Santa Ana Pueblo, 1899.*
Another fine example of pueblo mission architecture, this building was constructed about 1734 under the direction of Friar Diego Arias de Espinosa. These post-Revolt churches were built by local villagers, but usually not under the direction of the church fathers; rather it was the Spanish military authorities that supervised construction, and often the expenses were borne by private individuals.

147. *Interior, mission church at Santa Ana Pueblo. 1899.*

148. *Governor Manuel Salvadina Trujillo of San Juan Pueblo. 1899.*
The Spanish surnames of most Indians in the Rio Grande pueblos are a survival from the Spanish period and recall the days when most of the pueblos spoke Spanish as a second language. Today English is rapidly taking over as the second language, and many pueblo residents speak no Spanish at all.

149. *Daughter of Governor Trujillo. San Juan Pueblo, 1899.*
Vroman notes on the negative sleeve: "Of whom I bought buckskin boots."

150. *"Woman with Olla on Head, and Little Boy." San Juan Pueblo, 1899.*
Vroman bought the olla to add to his collection. There was little pottery work going on at San Juan at the time Vroman visited; however, the ware made then was of the type that has since become highly prized: polished red or black vessels without painted decoration. Maria Martinez of San Ildefonso brought this style to perfection. At San Juan the preference is for the red ware, highly polished as in the example in this picture. An occasional San Juan pot displays a textured surface, achieved by adding small lumps of clay to the finished pot.

151. *Taos Pueblo. 1899.*
Taos is the "classic" pueblo of the schoolbooks and probably the

most frequently visited by tourists in the Southwest. This imposing pyramid of apartments rises in one section to a height of seven stories. It was to this pueblo that Popé, a member of the San Juan community and a medicine man, came in 1680 to begin his organization, which would overthrow the Spanish conquerors. The revolt actually started at Taos and was so well organized among all the pueblos along the Rio Grande that in a matter of some two months the Spanish were either killed or expelled from the region. Reconquest did not take place until thirteen years later, though several attempts were made in the interim.

The Taoseños are a conservative people. In spite of their closeness to the modern town of Taos and the fact that their village is more or less constantly being visited by white tourists, these people have remained remarkably faithful to their ancient ways. Exposure to another culture has had minimum effect, and today the Taos people are leaders in the movement to restore the ceremonial life of the old times.

One major victory was won recently when the United States Government returned the sacred Blue Lake to tribal custody. Blue Lake was taken over by the U.S. Forest Service many years ago and had been a source of contention with the Taos people ever since. This lovely lake, of deep religious significance, lies in the wild mountain country that forms the dramatic backdrop in this photograph of the village.

152. *Estufa. Taos Pueblo, 1899.*

153. *Taos man and woman. 1899.*

117

118

119

120

121

122

123

126

128

157

129

130

131

132

133

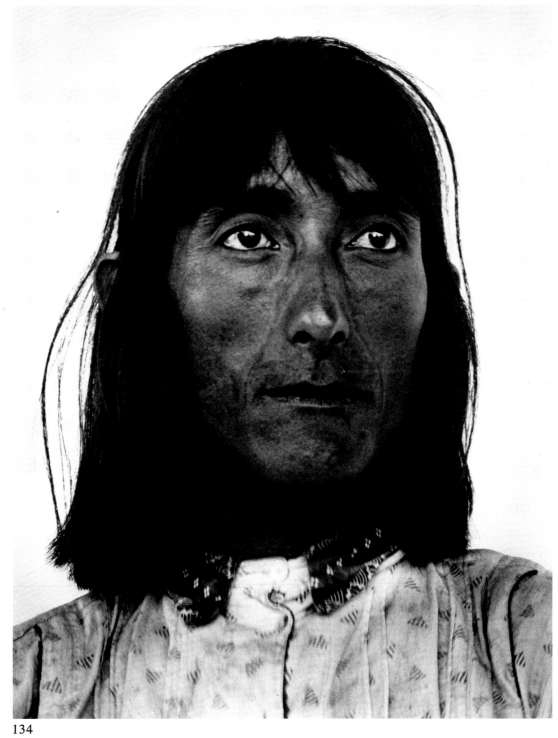

134

135

136

137

138

139

140

141

142

143

144

145

146

147

148

149

151

152

175

153

THE NAVAJOS

THE NAVAJOS are "newcomers" to the Southwest. Their ancestral home appears to have been the Pacific Northwest, since they speak a tongue derived from the Athapaskan language spoken in that area. They began to settle in the Southwest, first in small family units, around the middle of the sixteenth century. As more and more families came, and as individuals and families from other tribes, Pueblos especially, joined them, they developed a rich and distinctive complexity in language, religion, and life-style.

The region first settled by the Navajos was in the area of the upper Rio Grande and San Juan rivers, where there were a few scattered pueblo settlements. The Spanish had already arrived in the south, some one hundred years earlier, and the horse and the sheep had been introduced to the pueblo people. The Navajos have always shown remarkable gifts for assimilating useful practices from the surrounding cultures, and the domestication of sheep and horses opened for them new opportunities for rapid growth and expansion. They began to spread quickly over much of the country—what is today northern New Mexico and northeastern Arizona—tending their small bands of sheep, raising occasional crops of corn, and developing a richly eclectic creation mythology, a new medicine based upon the local plants and animals, and a deeply meaningful and expressive body of religious ceremonials.

The Navajos prospered in their new lands and in time began to feel the pressures of population growth against the limited resources available to them. They took to raiding the settled communities of the Pueblos and the Spanish, plundering mainly for horses and livestock. Meanwhile, in retaliation, the Spanish would raid the Navajos, not only to recover what had been taken from them, but to capture some healthy Navajo youths that could be sold as slaves. This kind of warfare waxed and waned all during the Spanish period.

In 1846 the United States Government took control of the Southwest, and more strenuous attempts were made to suppress the Navajo raiders. Several treaties were negotiated, to be broken without ever having really been put into effect. The Americans assumed that signatures meant something . . . at least that the *other* side would conform. But the Navajos were not part of anything that could conceivably be called a nation; they were simply a large number of totally autonomous clans with minimal political structure. Nothing a leader from one clan might do would be binding on another.

Grievances accumulated on each side. Navajos continued to plunder the Pueblo and white settlements; whites continued to take Navajos in slavery. So vexing had the whole situation become by 1863 that the Government decided the only solution was to round up all the Navajos and settle them elsewhere. In charge of this program was the famous scout Christopher "Kit" Carson. At this time there were probably some ten thousand Navajos widely scattered over a vast territory, much of it virtually inaccessible, with often forbidding climatic conditions. As the miltary forces under Carson began to fan out into the territory, the Navajos fled deeper into the hidden canyons and remote country, leaving behind livestock and homes. To counter this tactic, Carson resorted to a kind of scorched-earth policy, burning crops and homes, destroying herds, hoping to force the Navajo into starvation and submission.

As groups would surrender from time to time, they were herded into concentration camps. Some fell victim to massacres, others were taken and sold into slavery. Many died from exposure and malnutrition.

Finally, nearly nine thousand were rounded up and put into a forced march some three hundred miles to the southeast. Without provisions of the type to which they were accustomed, destitute of clothing, they suffered hardships during this march that are staggering to the imagination. Eventually they were led into the Bosque Redondo, forty square miles of arid wasteland on the side of the Pecos River. This was to be their new home.

This relocation was foredoomed to failure. Of all lands totally unsuitable for human habitation, the Bosque Redondo must certainly represent one of the worst. Attempts were made to grow some crops, but the water from the Pecos at this point was so mineralized that even the first crop was scrawny and insufficient, and succeeding crops failed altogether. The Navajos deteriorated steadily, wracked with malnutrition, venereal disease, and incredible suffering.

After four years of misery the utterly botched program was thankfully abandoned, and, under new treaties, the Navajos were allowed to return to the westernmost portion of their former homelands, remote now from any white settlements. Except for a sporadic raid and a steady encroachment upon the lands of the Hopis, the Navajos settled down to being good neighbors.

Since their confinement to the reservation the Navajos have grown to be the largest Indian tribe in the United States. Their weaving and their silverwork is appreciated and widely sought around the world. Royalties paid to the tribe from mineral exploitation on their reservation lands has enriched the tribal treasury and enabled the establishment of schools, craft fairs, a radio station, and other amenities. Still, many of the people continue with a wandering life, tending small herds of sheep and living by choice much as they did in the past.

In very recent years a new scourge, though, has come to Navajo land. In its insatiable need for more and more electric power to expand its population, Los Angeles is now drawing power from a huge coal-burning plant located near Farmington, New Mexico. The coal is being taken from an immense strip-mining operation on Black Mesa, territory held jointly by Navajos and Hopis. The land is scheduled for total devastation; the power plant spews dust and fumes over a huge area of the Navajo reservation; smog and frustration and deterioration of the quality of life increases for those unfortunate enough to have to live in Los Angeles. . . . What for?

It is better to look back at the Vroman years!

154. *Navajos and hogans. Bitahooche, 1895.*
On their way into the Hopi villages to see the snake dance in 1895, Vroman's party stopped briefly at this Navajo settlement. He writes in his notebook that here he made his first exposures of "the first real Indian houses I had ever seen."

155. *Interior of hogan. Bitahooche, 1897.*
Standing, in the back, left to right, are F. L. Monsen, of Albany, New York; Mr. Eggers, the driver of the buckboard; Vroman; and H. E. Hoyt, of Chicago. The whites seated on the floor are not identified. True to custom the Navajo ladies seat themselves at the north, the men at the south of the hogan. All true hogans have their entrance pointing eastward.

It is interesting to note that Vroman appears not to have used flash powder in making his interior photographs, relying instead upon the "available light."

156. *Navajo women weaving and spinning. 1901.*
For a long time it was assumed that Navajos learned the art of weaving from the Pueblo Indians. Recent scholarship suggests that this is not so, and that the Navajos brought a refined art with them when they migrated from the north. Weaving was a very highly developed craft among the tribes of the Northwest, where exceedingly complex tapestries were often made. It does appear, however, that many of the designs and some of the religious symbolism came from the contact with the Pueblos.

157. *"Navajo Woman at Loom, Holding Comb." 1901.*
This remarkably informative photograph shows all the parts and functioning of the Navajo loom. Weaving by this method involves long stretches of time, so the Navajo loom is made to be easily dismantled and moved from place to place while the work is still in progress. Such moving about is part of the Navajo life-style, with its dependence upon sheepherding.

158. *"Navajo Woman Weaving Todetsi Blanket." 1901.*
Vroman became an avid collector of Navajo blankets, often purchasing them before they were completed and having them sent to him later. He was particularly fond of the old bayetas when he could find them. These were woven from raveled yarns taken out of European imported fabrics. Only in this way were the weavers able to get the brilliant red yarns they liked so much. Very few of these blankets were to be found even in Vroman's time; today they are virtually priceless.

In his later years Vroman sold much of his blanket collection to the American Museum of Natural History and the Metropolitan Museum, eleven bayetas going to each.

159. *"Navajo Woman Cleaning Blanket." 1901.*
The title on the negative sleeve, repeated where the photograph has been reproduced in a couple of books on Navajo blankets, probably is an error. The blanket shown is a Germantown blanket, made from factory-spun wool that is sufficiently clean not to need further cleaning before it is sold.

A more likely explanation for the burying of the blanket is that it was warped out of shape as it came off the loom and was in need of "blocking" to straighten it. Covered with damp sand for a few days, it would very likely develop a "set" that would flatten it.

160. *Navajo woman roasting corn. 1901.*
In this method of roasting ears a small hollow is dug in the ground and a fire built in it. When the fire has died down it is scraped to one side. The corn ears are then dropped into the heated depression and covered with additional hot sand.

161. *Navajo silversmith working bellows. 1901.*
This is part of an extensive "how-to" series that Vroman made on silver-working, most of the negatives of which are lost.

162. *Navajo silversmith bending bracelets. 1901.*
The forge is seen to the right with a ladle on top of it, and with a large bellows just visible behind the man. The stone leaning on the forge is a mold carved from sandstone, into which molten silver is poured.

163. *Two Navajo women wearing Pendleton blankets. 1901.*

164. *Navajo man, Will, his wife and baby. 1901.*
The elaborate cradleboard into which babies were bound served as a convenience for carrying the children about. These boards are equipped with several appliances, such as a canopy to keep out sun or rain, trinkets and rattles to provide amusement, and a pillow that was so used as to result in some head-flattening.

Lewis and Clark in their early explorations noted the excellent postures and well-proportioned bodies of the Indians. This had been attributed to having been raised on a cradleboard. But modern reaction to this swaddling technique as a denial of freedom to move has resulted in its abandonment among many of the Indians.

Even more recently, though, it has been discovered that the sleeping habits developed by infants raised on cradleboards are very helpful in producing even teeth and a good "bite," as well as good proportion and posture.

165. *Portrait of Navajo man. 1903.*
Charles Lummis invited many of his Indian friends to attend the Pasadena Tournament of Roses Parade on New Year's Day, 1903. At the conclusion of the parade all went to El Alisal, Lummis' new and still uncompleted home in Highland Park. Vroman was on hand to make portraits of the visitors, nearly all of whom were Navajos. Hopis had been invited, but the superintendent of the reservation had refused to let any of them leave. Many of the Navajos appeared in flamboyant costumes that must have caused just as much of a stir at the parade as any of the floats going by.

166. *Hostine Martine, Navajo at Charles Lummis' party. 1903.*

167. *Navajo warrior "Many Arrows." 1903.*

168. *Navajo woman and baby. 1901.*

169. *Navajo man "Coyote." 1901.*

170. *Hostine Naz, Navajo man. 1901.*

171. *Navajo man "Jim." 1901.*

172. *"Charles' grandfather," Navajo man photographed near Keam's Canyon. 1901.*

173. *Navajo children on way to school. 1901.*

154

155

156

157

184

158

159

160

187

161

162

163

164

165

166

191

167

168

169

170

171

172

173

3 | APPENDICES

CHRONOLOGY

1856 Born April 15, at La Salle, Illinois.

1872 Left home, went to work.

1874 Employed by Chicago, Burlington and Quincy Railroad in capacities of operator, ticket-seller, dispatcher, agent.

1883 Begins collection of Japanese netsuke.

1892 Begins to make landscape photographs around Rockford, Illinois, using 5 x 7 plate camera. Traveled to and made photographs at Natural Bridge, Virginia. Married Esther H. Griest and moved to Pasadena, California.

1894 In August photographs at Niagara Falls, Gettysburg, Salt Lake City. Death of Mrs. Vroman in September, at Flora Dale, Pennsylvania. On November 14 opens bookstore with J. S. Glasscock at 60 E. Colorado Street, Pasadena.

1895 Acquires 6½ x 8½ plate camera and begins photography around Pasadena: Mt. Wilson, Sturdevant Camp, Altadena, Tournament of Roses Parade. Began series of *Ramona* illustrations at Camulos Rancho. In August made first visit to Hopi village of Walpi, photographing snake ceremony. Also photographed at Sichimovi, Tewa (Hano); Navajo hogans at Bitahoochee; Petrified Forest. Members of party: H. N. Rust, Mr. Crandall, and Mrs. Love. Print exhibition in Pasadena.

1896 Photography at Guajome Rancho for *Ramona* series; missions in Southern California; pack-trip to Mt. Wilson, Rubio, and Eaton Canyons.

1897 Extended tour, beginning May 15 and ending about September 4, up the California coast to San Francisco by buckboard and stagecoach, photographing all of the missions en route and miscellaneous views around Monterey and San Francisco; thence by rail to Illinois and Pennsylvania, photographing around his family home in Rockford, Illinois, and at Media, Pennsylvania; returning to Chicago and inviting Mr. H. E. Hoyt to accompany him to snake ceremony at Walpi. By August in Arizona, joined with Mr. S. L. Munsun of Albany, New York. Photographing around First Mesa Hopi villages, including snake ceremony on August 21. Made first visit to Hopi Second Mesa villages, photographing in Mishongnovi for a single afternoon. Later toured Walnut Canyon; Grand Canyon; Petrified Forest; pueblos of Zuñi, Laguna, Acoma; making extensive series of photographs. At Laguna met Dr. Frederick Webb Hodge and was invited to accompany Hodge as photographer on expedition to make first climb of Katsimo.

1898 Led tour for eleven days to Hopi villages, visiting Second Mesa, photographing snake ceremony at Third Mesa village of Oraibi. Navajo Gallo Races photographed. In party: Dr. M. R. Harned from Illinois; Professor Burton Holmes, the travel lecturer and writer; Miss Duggan (Rattlesnake Jack); Mr. Studd; Mr. Kizzley; Mr. DePew; and Mrs. H. H. Cole.

1899 Spent seven weeks in Rio Grande pueblos, making photographs of the missions on a special assignment from Dr. F. W. Hodge. Photographed ruins in Frijoles Canyon. In party: Dr. Hodge, George Parker Winship, Dr. Elliot Coues. In California continued with *Ramona* photographs.

1900 Visited East Coast, photographing in Library of Congress, and in Media, Pennsylvania. In summer visited all three Hopi mesas, photographing snake ceremony at Oraibi and flute ceremony at Mishongnovi. Additional photography at Walpi and Shipaulovi. Photographed again around Katsimo, but did not climb the mesa. Visited and photographed in Zuñi, Acoma, Isleta. In party: John Gunn, J. W. O'Hara, Dr. M. R. Harned, D. H. Kendall, J. E. Pectu.

1901 Joined the Museum-Gates Expedition, under leadership of Peter Goddard Gates, from July 17 to August 30. Photographs of archaeological digs in Navajo country. Visited Oraibi, Sichimovi, and photographed snake ceremony at Walpi and Mishongnovi. Many photographs of Navajos. Made series of photographs of Yosemite Valley, including small Indian colony. Publication of articles in *Photo-Era* about making photographs in the Southwest.

1902 Visited all Hopi villages, photographing flute ceremony at Mishongnovi and snake ceremony at Oraibi. Toured Isleta, Acoma, Zuñi. Long series of cloud pictures made on way to Grand Canyon and Petrified Forest. Members of party: H. E. Hoopes and G. J. Kuhrts, of Pasadena, and Homer (?).

1903 New Year's Day made photographs of Navajos at home of Charles Lummis in Los Angeles. Traveled to Orient, visiting both China and Japan.

1904 Visited all Hopi villages, Zuñi, Acoma, Laguna. Photographed inscriptions at El Morro. First trip to Cañon de Chelly. Members of party: Mr. B. O. Kendall, Miss Kendall, Dr. and Mrs. M. R. Harned, Lora Harned.

1909 Traveled to Orient with stop in Hawaii. Also trip to Canadian Rockies.

1910 Trip to Canada.

1911 Traveled to East Coast, visited John Burroughs.

1912 Trip to Europe, sailing on S. S. *Rotterdam*, in party with F. N. Finney of South Pasadena and Milwaukee, Miss Ranold, and Miss Ranold's niece. Toured valley of the Loire, photographing village scenes and the châteaux, Switzerland, and the Rhine Valley, all by automobile.

1914 Trip to Canadian Rockies with F. N. Finney, trip to East Coast, making his last photographs at Cape Cod.

1916 On July 24 died at home of George Howell in Altadena, of intestinal cancer. Survived by his mother, two sisters, and three half-sisters.

VROMAN'S TECHNIQUE

Throughout the ten-year period of his most serious work in photography, Vroman made principal use of a 6½″ × 8½″ plate camera, fitted with several top-quality anastigmatic lenses. He supplemented this basic equipment with a 5″ × 7″ back, and a 5″ × 8″ back for the 6½″ × 8½″ camera, and also seems to have carried a 4″ × 5″ view camera using film-based negative material or plates. From time to time he also used hand cameras.

On the trip to Mishongnovi about 1901 he photographed parts of the snake ceremony with a panorama camera using roll film and a rotating lens. The inventory of the collection in the Los Angeles County Museum shows a series of 10″ × 12″ plates of California missions and of the Library of Congress, undated. These negatives have been lost.

In general it can be said that Vroman's equipment differed very little from that used today by the large format worker. He had the obvious handicap of the glass plate negative, which increased weight and bulk. But his camera was complete with swings and tilts and interchangeable lens boards and backs, and except for minor inconveniences would have been a very acceptable instrument in the hands of an Edward Weston.

Vroman did most of his own processing, sometimes assisted by his friend Crandall, in a darkroom in his upstairs apartment at 168 East Colorado Street in Pasadena. On the roof of this building he exposed his platinum and solio papers to the sun, using as many as three 9″ × 12″ printing frames at one time, each masked down to 6″ × 8″. He rarely cropped any of his plates, though this does not seem to have been a matter of strict discipline with him. When he had his work published, much cropping—often to odd shapes—and vignetting was done, without evidence that Vroman raised much protest. He also sent out his lantern-slide plates for hand-coloring. However, for his own use and for the prints that he gave away, he adhered to the "straight" print, sharp with a full scale of tones. There is no evidence that he made enlargements, though enlarging was a well-established, if laborious, technique during his time. Even his 4″ × 5″ images were contact-printed, though the main use for negatives of this size seems to have been to make lantern slides. On most of his trips ot Indian country he carried not only his 6½″ × 8½″ view camera, but the 4″ × 5″ as well, and on many occasions a 5″ × 7″ camera. He often duplicated his subjects, using as many as three sizes for some. Thus, if for any reason one negative failed, he very often had backup with another.

Vroman did his plate developing in a then popular Eikonogen-Pyro formula, timing by inspection. The plates used were M.A. Seed

Dry Plates and Cramer Isochromatic. These were orthochromatic in sensitivity and permitted cloud photographs, to which Vroman was much devoted, by the use of fairly deep yellow color screens.

Some years after he had discontinued using the large plate camera, favoring instead a small hand camera for his journeys to the Orient and Europe, Vroman undertook a massive project of copying all of his plates onto 5″ × 7″ sheet film, creating a set of transparent positives on film of all his work up through 1904. It is presumed this was done to preserve the collection, since there had already been some casualties among the glass plates. For the purpose of making these copies, he secured a special enlarging and copying camera. These positives are now in the Los Angeles Museum collection. For the most part they are of good quality and have made it possible at times for us to recover images that have been lost due to missing or broken original plates.

In presenting the selection in this book we have had to rely on modern prints, made from the original negatives, or duplicate negatives. Very few original "vintage" Vroman prints survive, and these few rarely lend themselves to reproduction. In making these modern prints we have been guided less by the platinotypes than by the solio prints that we have been privileged to examine, largely because the very long range and general softness of the platinotypes is difficult to reproduce; and on the other hand, the surface and tonal characteristics of the solio papers are more like those of our modern papers, and reproduce well.

We have taken many liberties with cropping, and in a handful of cases may have done unintentional violence to Vroman's concepts— if he had them—of doing all his cropping on the ground glass. We feel justified in this practice since now and then we think we have come up with a stronger composition.

The appendix offers a listing of the negative source for each of the reproductions.

Equipment:

Carlton camera, tripod, 1 plate holder, case	$45.00
five 6½″ × 8½″ plate holders	12.00
four 5″ × 8″ plate holders	8.00
one 5″ × 8″ back for 6½″ × 8½″	6.00
six kits	1.80
one leather case	2.00
one tripod case	1.25
one 6½″ × 8½″ Zeiss series IIa lens	54.00
one B & L shutter for above lens	15.00
one 6½″ × 8½″ Zeiss series V lens	28.00
one 5″ × 8″ Zeiss series IIIa lens	35.00
one B & L shutter for same	15.00
one 4″ × 5″ Stenheil lens No. 21704	20.00
one B & L shutter for same	12.00
one 4″ × 5″ wide-angle lens	10.00
three Buch flanges	1.00
	$266.05

VROMAN'S INVENTORY OF EQUIPMENT AND SUPPLIES, 1895

Printing and Developing Fixtures:

two 10″ × 12″ printing frames	$2.00
two 8″ × 10″ printing frames	1.50
two 6½″ × 8½″ printing frames	1.20
three 5″ × 8″ printing frames	1.65
one 8″ × 10″ tray	1.25
two 6½″ × 8½″ trays	1.80
one 6½″ × 8½″ PM tray	.70
two glass PM trays	.50
one 9″ × 14″ iron tray	.60
200 6½″ × 8½″ negative preservers	1.00
100 5″ × 8″ negative preservers	.50
100 5″ × 7″ negative preservers	.50
100 4″ × 5″ negative preservers	.30
one Negative rack	.40
one 8-oz. graduate	.40
one 4-oz. graduate	.30
one 1-oz. graduate	.15
one 1-min. graduate	.20
one Robinson trimmer	.40

one LS mat shaper	.40
one dark lantern	1.50
one LS wash box	1.00
	$18.25

Chemicals, supplies, etc.:

Chemicals, etc., on hand	$5.00
five doz. Exc. plates 6½″ × 8½″	5.00
two doz. Exc. plates 5″ × 8″	1.50
three doz. Exc. plates 4″ × 5″	1.20
one doz. Seed NH 6½″ × 8½″ plates	2.10
ten doz. Eastman LS plates	5.00
	$19.80

AS OF APRIL 1:

Lumber for tables and shelving in darkroom	$5.00

ADDITIONAL EQUIPMENT ADDED AFTER JANUARY 1:

one canvas plate holder	$2.00
six 6½″ × 8½″ plate holders	14.40
one level	1.00
one 3″ Carhett color screen	2.00
one focusing glass	.80
one focusing cloth	.75
one Light Anthony 4 fold tripod	5.00
	$25.95

Chemicals, supplies, etc.:

two doz. Seed 6½″ × 8½″ plates	$2.80
one doz. Seed 5″ × 8″ plates	1.00
one gross BP Red Label 6½″ × 8½″ plates	4.00
C. L. Crandall devel. print, Tone	3.00
	$10.80

AS OF APRIL 27:

Chemicals, supplies, etc.:

one gross 6″ × 8″ BP paper	$3.00
one doz. 6½″ × 8½″ WK platinotype	——

one doz. 4″ × 6″ WK platinotype	——
one doz. 4″ × 6″ plat mounts	——
one doz. 6½″ × 8½″ plat mounts	——
	$3.00

AS OF JULY 1:

Chemicals, supplies, etc.:

three doz. Seed 6½″ × 8½″ plates	$3.75
one doz. BP Mat paper 6½″ × 8½″	.50
one doz. Aristo plat 6½″ × 8½″	.50
200 6½″ × 8½″ mts.	2.50
100 5″ × 7″ mts.	1.00
100 5″ × 8″ mts.	1.00
100 4″ × 5″ mts.	.50
twelve plat mts.	1.50
blotters	.25
blue print	.20
plain Saxe paper	.50
one doz. platino paper	.60
Crandall developer for platinotype	.50
Crandall doz. cab photos	1.00
	$14.30

AS OF JULY 25:

Chemicals, supplies, etc:

one gross 6½″ × 8½″ Aristo paper	$3.25

THE VROMAN COLLECTIONS

During his lifetime Vroman's photographs were fairly well distributed and known by the public. He had published a few articles, which he illustrated with his own photographs; he sold prints to companies, such as the Detroit Photographic Company, that published tourist views and brochures, usually hand-coloring the prints and retouching them extensively before reproducing them; he used his photographs to illustrate an edition of Helen Hunt Jackson's *Ramona*; he published a deck of playing cards featuring Indian subjects, which he hoped would win sympathy for Indian rights among the white socialites; he lectured widely on Indians and the West, using lantern slides of his own making; and from time to time he mounted various exhibitions of his platinum prints. Contemporary newspaper announcements often referred to him as the "artist-photographer."

Upon Vroman's death in 1916 this extensive body of work passed into near oblivion. In spite of the fairly widespread circulation of his output, he never came to be recognized on the East Coast by the photographic-artistic establishment. He had not published in the magazines or the several annuals promoting photography as "art." He belonged to no organized groups of photographers outside of a small and informal "camera club" that he had himself started in Pasadena. In short, there was no one nor any group prepared to continue the presentation of his photographs.

His personal collection of negatives was sold to the Audio-Visual Department of the Los Angeles County Board of Education. It is possible that at the time the collection was in some state of disarray, for the school system undertook a complete renumbering and cataloging of the negatives. This process was perhaps more damaging than helpful, serving to confuse the chronological ordering that Vroman's numbering system achieved and the identification of many of the subjects, and causing the loss of much valuable information and annotation of the collection.

Because the school system was ill-equipped to manage the collection some serious breakage of the glass plates occurred and deterioration from chemical residues and fungus set in. Had it not been for the discovery of the collection by Lawrence Clark Powell in the late 1950s and its subsequent transfer to the Los Angeles County Museum of Natural History the collection would perhaps have finally disintegrated and been thrown out as so much useless glass.

Ruth I. Mahood, who was, at the time of the transfer of the plates, in charge of the Department of History at the Museum, took a great interest in the discovery of the old plates. She had a number of them printed and opened a permanent Vroman gallery at the museum, where many fine enlargements of the negatives are on view and where various pieces of Vroman memorabilia have now been gathered, including cameras and other equipment that he used.

The first modern publication of Vroman's work was the issuance in 1961 of *Photographer of the Southwest, Adam Clark Vroman, 1856–1916*, by Ruth I. Mahood, with an introduction by Beaumont Newhall. (Los Angeles: Ward Ritchie Press).

On several of the expeditions that Vroman accompanied as photographer he made duplicate sets of negatives, one for his personal collection, one for the expedition archives. The negatives made in 1901 for the Museum-Gates Expedition are now, in part at least, in the collection of the Southwest Museum in Los Angeles.

Publications of the Bureau of Ethnology have from time to time made use of Vroman photographs that are in its collections. It is not known whether original negatives exist there.

Some negatives of the European trip of 1912 and the Canadian trip of 1914 were among Vroman's personal effects that were removed from the bookstore in later years. Plans are now being made to have these negatives accessioned in a collection where use can be made of them. A fairly large collection of small roll-film negatives on nitrate-base film, possibly made in 1903, has deteriorated so severely that it cannot be used any longer. This collection turned up in the possession of a commercial photographer in Pasadena.

The Vroman negatives are of special importance since few of his own prints are known today. A single, more or less complete collection of his prints, all platinotypes, bound in sixteen leather volumes, are in the possession of the Pasadena Public Library. This set was printed by Vroman in his last years, long after he had ceased his travels in the Southwest. As a result, the set suffers from omissions of information and errors in identification and negative numbering, but nevertheless is invaluable for the information it does provide and for insight into his approach to printing. This collection offers the only opportunity for seeing the Vroman oeuvre intact for the ten-year period 1895–1904.

Occasional prints that can be safely attributed to Vroman appear in various other collections. Some platinum and solio prints, a few scrapbooks of small prints from the Canadian and European trips, and lantern slides used in his lectures are part of the Vroman material held by Mrs. Hazel Wiedmann, Vroman's niece.

Selections of modern prints of many of the Vroman negatives are now included in collections at the George Eastman House, Rochester, New York; the University of California, Riverside; and the University Art Museum at the University of New Mexico, Albuquerque.

SOURCES OF
THE PHOTOGRAPHS

The following listing of photographs indicates the source of the reproduction prints used in making the plates for this book. Most of the prints are direct-contact prints, made on silver chloride paper, using the original 6½″ × 8½″ glass-plate negatives, and in these cases no special annotation is given. The V numbers refer to the negatives in the collection of the Los Angeles County Museum; the SWM numbers are those of the Southwest Museum. Other sources are individually indicated. Numbers in parentheses are those assigned to the negatives by Vroman and were not available in all cases.

Frontispiece. Enlarged from 5″ × 7″ negative. Collection of Sudworth Sheldon.
Page 2. Silver print from 4″ × 5″ negative. Collection Los Angeles County Museum. 1895.
Page 3. Platinum print reduced from 6½″ × 8½″ negative. Private collection. 1900 (?).
Page 16. Platinum print by ACV. Private collection. 1904.
Page 18. Platinum print by ACV reduced from 6½″ × 8½″ negative. Private collection. 1902.
Page 20. Enlarged from frame 35 × 45 mm. sprocket-holed motion picture negative film.
Page 23. Platinum prints reduced from 8″ × 10″ negative. Private collection. 1902 (?).
1. SWM-4627 solio print
2. V-516 (626) enlarged from duplicate 6½″ × 8½″ negative
3. V-517 (628) contact print from duplicate negative
4. SWM-4504
5. V-509 (620)
6. V-508 (618)
7. V-1635 (1204)
8. V-512 (622) contact print from duplicate negative
9. V-511 (621)
10. Platinum print by ACV. Private collection.
11. V-1032 (C12) enlarged portion 5″ × 7″ negative
12. V-1099 (C38) enlarged portion 5″ × 7″ negative
13. V-1045 (C45) enlarged portion 5″ × 7″ negative
14. V-2366 (1011) enlarged portion 6½″ × 8½″ negative
15. SWM-4520 enlarged portion 6½″ × 8½″ negative
16. V-1588 (C33) enlarged portion 5″ × 7″ negative
17. SWM-4307
18. Platinum print by ACV. Private collection.
19. SWM-4462 enlarged portion 5″ × 7″ negative

20. V-2376 (C26) enlarged from 5″ × 7″ negative
21. V-1130 (C183) enlarged from 5″ × 7″ negative
22. V-1124 (C177) enlarged portion of 5″ × 7″ negative
23. V-1140 (C193) enlarged portion of 5″ × 7″ negative
24. SWM-4554
25. V-2365 (1010)
26. SWM 4503 contact print from duplicate negative
27. SWM 4499 contact print from duplicate negative
28. V528 contact print from duplicate negative
29. V-1445 (1286) contact print from duplicate negative
30. V-560 (22)
31. V-676-A (1263) Copy of print in collection of Robert Pearce Myers. The original negative has been lost and the transparent positive in the Los Angeles Museum collection is very poor.
32. V-554 from enlarged negative made from 5″ × 7″ interpositive
33. V-559 (21) reduced from 6½″ × 8½″ negative
34. V-556 (19) reduced from 6½″ × 8½″ negative
35. SWM 4660 reduced from 6½″ × 8½″ negative
36. SWM-4492 solio print reduced from 6½″ × 8½″ negative
37. V-716 (24½) enlarged negative made from 5″ × 7″ interpositive
38. SWM-4510 enlarged portion of 5″ × 7″ negative
39. V-679 (1266) reduced print from 6½″ × 8½″ duplicate negative.
40. V-2358
41. V-596 (65)
42. V-2356
43. SWM-4319
44. SWM-no number
45. V-1011 reduced from 6½″ × 8½″ negative
46. SWM-4483 reduced from 6½″ × 8½″ negative
47. V-633 (1140)
48. SWM-4308 reduced from 6½″ × 8½″ negative
49. SWM-4309 reduced from 6½″ × 8½″ negative
50. SWM-4310 reduced from 6½″ × 8½″ negative
51. SWM-4311 reduced from 6½″ × 8½″ negative
52. SWM-4312 reduced from 6½″ × 8½″ negative
53. SWM-4313 reduced from 6½″ × 8½″ negative
54. SWM-4704 reduced from 6½″ × 8½″ negative
55. SWM-4705 reduced from 6½″ × 8½″ negative
56. V-678 (1265)
57. V-603 (73) Platinum print by ACV. Private collection.
58. SWM-4323 (653)
59. V-1719 (18½)
60. SWM-4646 reduced from 6½″ × 8½″ negative
61. V-602 (72½) reduced from 6½″ × 8½″ negative
62. V-1028 (C8) enlarged from 5″ × 7″ negative
63. SWM-4529
64. V-653 (1233) enlarged from portion of 5″ × 7″ negative
65. V-542 from portion of 5″ × 7″ negative
66. V-607 (77) reduced from 6½″ × 8½″ negative
67. V-612 (82)
68. V-537 (653) enlarged portion of 6½″ × 8½″ duplicate negative
69. SWM-4513 portion of 4″-wide panorama negative on nitrate base
70. Platinum print by ACV. Private collection.
71. V-617 (87)
72. V-647 (1225) reduced from 6½″ × 8½″ negative
73. V-645 (1223) reduced from 6½″ × 8½″ negative
74. V-625 (95)
75. V-545 (660) reduced from 6½″ × 8½″ negative
76. SWM-4551 reduced from 6½″ × 8½″ negative
77. V-638 (1208) enlarged negative made from 5″ × 7″ interpositive
78. V-702 (1299-F) enlarged negative from 5″ × 7″ interpositive
79. V-520 (637) reduced print from 6½″ × 8½″ duplicate negative
80. V-629 (99) portion of 6½″ × 8½″ negative
81. V-571 (37) contact print from duplicate negative
82. V-574 (40) contact print from duplicate negative
83. V-705 (1181) reduced from 6½″ × 8½″ negative
84. V-573 (39) portion 6½″ × 8½″ negative
85. V-575 (41) contact print from duplicate negative
86. V-585 (51) contact print from duplicate negative
87. V-576 (42)
88. V-577 (43)
89. V-579 (45)
90. V-587 (53) contact print from duplicate negative
91. SWM-268 (G123-28)
92. SWM-4509 reduced from 6½″ × 8½″ negative
93. SWM-4510 reduced from 6½″ × 8½″ negative
94. Robert Pearce Myers collection. Copy of silver print.
95. V-538 (653)

96. V-864 (718) reduced from 6½″ × 8½″ negative
97. V-866 (722) reduced print from 6½″ × 8½″ duplicate negative
98. V-2361 (1070) enlarged portion of 6½″ × 8½″ negative
99. V-868 (724)
100. V-869 (725) contact print from duplicate negative
101. V-2382 enlarged portion of 5″ × 7″ negative
102. V-955 reduced from 6½″ × 8½″ negative
103. V-2392 enlarged portion of 5″ × 7″ negative
104. V-2389 (C211) enlarged portion of 5″ × 7″ negative
105. V-1105 (C157) enlarged portion of 5″ × 7″ negative
106. V-2414 (C207) enlarged portion of 5″ × 7″ negative
107. V-1060 (C64) enlarged portion of 5″ × 7″ negative
108. V-1061 (C65) enlarged portion of 5″ × 7″ negative
109. V-1059 (C63) enlarged portion of 5″ × 7″ negative
110. V-837 enlarged negative of portion of 6½″ × 8½″ interpositive
111. V-874 enlarged portion of 6½″ × 8½″ negative
112. V-879 (736)
113. V-878 (735) reduced portion of 6½″ × 8½″ negative
114. V-2290 (1073) reduced from 6½″ × 8½″ negative
115. V-2352 (1074) reduced from 6½″ × 8½″ negative
116. V-2381 (C55) from 5″ × 7″ interpositive
117. V-1617 (226)
118. V-904 (753) enlarged portion of duplicate negative, 6½″ × 8½″
119. V-917 (13-'02) contact print from duplicate negative
120. V-913 (774) reduced from 6½″ × 8½″ negative
121. V-1151 (C78) enlarged negative from 5″ × 7″ interpositive
122. V-947 (1593)
123. V-1073 (C169) enlarged from 5″ × 7″ negative
124. V-920 (17-'02)
125. V-921 (18-'02)
126. V-1612
127. V-1063 (C225) enlarged from 5″ × 7″ negative
128. V-1681 enlarged negative from 5″ × 7″ interpositive
129. V-1009 (902) reduced from 6½″ × 8½″ negative
130. V-1071 (C166) from 5″ × 7″ negative
131. V-893 (1-'02) reduced print from 6½″ × 8½″ duplicate negative
132. V-895 contact print from duplicate negative
133. V-1074 (C170) enlarged negative from 5″ × 7″ interpositive
134. V-2402 (C223) enlarged from 5″ × 7″ negative
135. V-2068 (849) enlarged portion 6½″ × 8½″ negative
136. V-2078 (858) contact print from duplicate negative
137. V-430
138. V-2051 (832) reduced from 6½″ × 8½″ negative
139. V-2054 (835) reduced from 6½″ × 8½″ negative
140. V-2059 (840) reduced from 6½″ × 8½″ negative
141. V-2058 (839) enlarged portion 6½″ × 8″ negative
142. V-1079 (C153) enlarged negative from 5″ × 7″ interpositive
143. V-1599 (C155) enlarged negative from 5″ × 7″ interpositive
144. V-2047 (828) contact print from duplicate negative
145. V-2049 (830) reduced from 6½″ × 8½″ negative
146. V-2091 reduced from 6½″ × 8½″ negative
147. V-2092 (874) reduced from 6½″ × 8½″ negative
148. V-1080 (C154) enlarged portion 5″ × 7″ negative
149. V-1097 (C149) enlarged negative from portion 5″ × 7″ interpositive
150. V-1548 (C152) enlarged portion 5″ × 7″ negative
151. V-2024 (4) reduced print from 6½″ × 8½″ duplicate negative
152. V-1007 (807) reduced print from 6½″ × 8½″ duplicate negative
153. V-1148 (C143) enlarged from 5″ × 7″ negative
154. V-710 (605) enlarged negative from 5″ × 7″ interpositive
155. V-711 (606) enlarged negative from 5″ × 7″ interpositive
156. SWM-4575
157. SWM-4570 solio print
158. SWM-4572 solio print
159. SWM-4573
160. SWM-4604 reduced from 6½″ × 8½″ negative
161. SWM-4586 reduced from 6½″ × 8½″ negative
162. SWM-4580 solio print
163. SWM-4605
164. SWM-4609
165. V-728 (45) from 5″ × 7″ interpositive
166. V-2359 (43) from 5″ × 7″ interpositive
167. V-1661 (53½)
168. SWM-4606
169. SWM-4659
170. V-1111 (C163) enlarged from 5″ × 7″ negative
171. V-1113 (C165) enlarged from 5″ × 7″ negative
172. SWM-4600 (1192)
173. SWM-4596

SELECTED READING LIST

Introduction

Belous, Russell E., and Weinstein, Robert A. *Will Soule: Indian Photographer At Fort Sill, 1869–1874*. Los Angeles: The Ward Ritchie Press, 1969.

Collier, John. *Indians of America*. New York: New American Library, 1947.

Forbes, Jack D. *The Indian in America's Past*. New York: Spectrum Books, 1964.

Hagan, William T. *American Indians*. Chicago: The University of Chicago Press, 1961.

Horan, James D. *Timothy H. O'Sullivan, America's Forgotten Photographer*. New York: Doubleday & Company, 1966.

Jackson, William Henry. *Time Exposure*. New York: G. P. Putnam's Sons, 1946.

Josephy, Alvin D. *The Indian Heritage of America*. New York: Bantam Books, 1969.

Lowie, Robert H. *Indians of the Plains*. New York: American Museum Science Books, 1963.

Mahood, Ruth I. *Photographer of the Southwest, Adam Clark Vroman, 1856–1916*. Los Angeles: The Ward Ritchie Press, 1961.

Newhall, Beaumont. *The History of Photography*. rev. ed. New York: Museum of Modern Art, 1964.

Taft, Robert. *Photography and the American Scene*. New York: The Macmillan Company, 1942.

The Pueblo Indians

Collier, John. *On the Gleaming Way*. Chicago: Swallow Books, 1949.

Courlander, Harold. *The Fourth World of the Hopis*. New York: Crown Publishers, 1971.

Dockstader, Frederick J. *The Kachina and the White Man*. Bloomfield Hills, Mich.: Cranbrook Institute of Science, 1954.

Dorsey, George A. *Indians of the Southwest*. Chicago: Atchison, Topeka & Santa Fe Railway System, 1903.

Dozier, Edward P. *The Pueblo Indians of North America*. New York: Holt, Rinehart and Winston, 1970.

Feder, Norman. *American Indian Art*. New York: Harry N. Abrams, 1971.

Fewkes, Jesse Walter. *Tusayan Snake Ceremonies*. Bureau of American Ethnology, Sixteenth Annual Report. Washington, 1894–95.

——— *Hopi Katcinas.* Bureau of American Ethnology, Twenty-first Annual Report. Washington, 1899–1900.

——— *Designs on Prehistoric Hopi Pottery.* Bureau of American Ethnology, Thirty-third Annual Report. Washington, 1911–12.

Forrest, Earle R. *The Snake Dance of the Hopi Indians.* Los Angeles: Westernlore Press, 1961.

Hodge, Frederick Webb, ed. *Handbook of American Indians North of Mexico.* Bureau of American Ethnology, 1906. Reprint. New York: Pageant Books, 1960.

Kubler, George. *The Religious Architecture of New Mexico.* Colorado Springs: Taylor Museum, 1940.

Lange, Charles H. *Cochiti, A New Mexico Pueblo, Past and Present.* Carbondale, Ill.: Southern Illinois University Press, 1968.

Lummis, Charles F. *Bullying the Moqui.* Prescott, Ariz.: Prescott College Press, 1968.

Mindeleff, Victor. *A Study of Pueblo Architecture in Tusayan and Cibola.* Bureau of American Ethnology, Eighth Annual Report. Washington, 1886–87.

Morgan, Lewis Henry. *Houses and House Life of the American Aborigines.* Washington: United States Department of Interior, 1881.

Nequatewa, Edmund. *The Truth of a Hopi.* Flagstaff, Ariz.: Northern Arizona Society of Science and Art, 1947.

Silverberg, Robert. *The Pueblo Revolt.* New York: Weybright and Talley, 1970.

Simmons, Leo W. *Sun Chief, The Autobiography of a Hopi Indian.* New Haven: Yale University Press, 1942.

Stevenson, James. *Illustrated Catalogue of the Collections Obtained from the Indians of New Mexico and Arizona in 1879.* Bureau of American Ethnology, Second Annual Report. Washington, 1880–81.

Stevenson, Matilda Cox, 1901–02, *The Zuñi Indians.* Bureau of American Ethnology, Twenty-third Annual Report. Washington, 1901–02. Reprint. Glorieta, N.M.: Rio Grande Press, 1970.

Waters, Frank. *Masked Gods.* Chicago: Swallow Press, 1950.

——— *Book of the Hopi.* New York: The Viking Press, 1963.

Yamada, George, ed. *The Great Resistance, a Hopi Anthology.* New York, privately printed, 1957.

The Navajos

Amsden, Charles Avery. *Navaho Weaving, Its Technic and History.* Santa Ana, Calif.: The Fine Arts Press, 1934. Reprint. Glorieta, N.M.: Rio Grande Press, 1969.

Gilpin, Laura. *The Enduring Navaho.* Austin: University of Texas Press, 1968.

Kahlenberg, Mary Hunt, and Berlant, Anthony. *The Navajo Blanket.* New York: Praeger Publishers, 1972.

Kluckhohn, Clyde, and Leighton, Dorothea. *The Navaho.* Cambridge: Harvard University Press, 1946.

Kluckhohn, Clyde; Hill, W.W.; and Kluckhohn, Lucy Wales. *Navaho Material Culture.* Cambridge: Harvard University Press, 1971.

Terrell, John Upton. *The Navajos.* New York: Weybright and Talley, 1970.

This book was set on the linotype in Times Roman by American Book Stratford Press. The display type is Weiss Initials II. It was printed on Warren's Paloma paper by Rapoport Printing Company using their Stonetone Process. The binding is by Sendor Bindery, Inc.
Designed by Jacqueline Schuman.